Angelos

Sixpence in Her Shoe

Also by Phyllis McGinley

ON THE CONTRARY

ONE MORE MANHATTAN

POCKETFUL OF WRY

HUSBANDS ARE DIFFICULT

STONES FROM A GLASS HOUSE

A SHORT WALK FROM THE STATION

THE LOVE LETTERS OF PHYLLIS MCGINLEY

MERRY CHRISTMAS, HAPPY NEW YEAR

THE PROVINCE OF THE HEART

TIMES THREE

Sixpence in Her Shoe

PHYLLIS McGINLEY

1964

FOR PATSY

for whom this book was written

Most of the material in this book originally appeared in the *Ladies Home Journal*. "Realms of Gilt" ("Talking Down Talked Down") originally appeared in *Glamour*.

Sixth Printing 1964

Contents

The Family

A Wreath of Recipes

1 ☙ An Unapologetic Preface

This is a book for, by, and about the American housewife.

I admit it as shamelessly as I confess that its title refers to an alien legend. For once upon a time, tales say, the good housewife of rustic England was likely, quite literally, to stumble upon a fortune. Provided she was clean, kind, thrifty, and industrious, she every now and then found sixpence in her shoe, left there stealthily as a sign of approbation by whichever sylvan deity inhabited her countryside.

So by sixpence I mean a reward. And it is the rewards as well as the challenges and difficulties of creating a home which I discuss here. But the book is about other things as well—about women in general and their odd enthusiasms; about myths, manners, moralities; about husbands; about guests, books, friends, children, food, the paraphernalia of living.

Somewhere along the way, too, it has turned into a kind of autobiography, which is no doubt natural since the experiences I have drawn on are largely my own. And that is also natural. By temperament I am a nest builder. I have other occupations, chiefly writing and the delights of conversation. Yet to keep a house is my native vocation and I consider it an honorable estate.

I add, though, a word of warning. When I speak of housekeeping I do not, of necessity, refer to housework. This is no manual on how to polish brass or clean ovens or have the whitest wash on the block. Being a housewife may or may not entail all those tasks; it has, at times, for me. But tasks is what they are, nothing more. They do not touch the heart of the matter. Whether one likes or loathes the daily round of chores, whether one personally wields a broom or leaves it to apter talents, has no bearing on my premise—that it is into the hands of women life has dropped its most significant duties.

THE WIFE

2 ❧ *The Oldest Profession*

God must love housewives as He does the poor, He makes so many of us. It may solace nobody to recall statistics. Yet (unless you believe the legend that there was originally a Lilith who tempted Adam before Eve married him) it is perfectly apparent that ours is not only the oldest profession in the world but the most numerous. It is not the daughters of Joy who are seniors of a calling, but we, the handmaids of the home.

Personally, I find it a comfortable idea. There is something soothing about the thought that I am one of an enormous, an antique sisterhood, each of us bent on much the same ends, all of us doing our able or our fumbling best to hold the planet steady on its axis by such primitive expedients as hanging window curtains, bandaging knees, or getting meals to the table on time.

Because we are so many, we are sometimes downgraded in our own eyes. We form no unions, belong to no professional organizations. We do not federate, lobby in the Senate, go on strike, scream for shorter working days, or establish corporations. Our hours are peculiar, our wages irregular. Few honors come to us in the shape of scrolls or Doctorates or Chairmanships of Foundations named with our names. If we have any public status apart from that which our husbands' abilities bring us, it is limited and local. Nobody has so far received a Pulitzer Prize for contriving a poetic boiled custard, in spite of the fact (which I know from experience) that it is a feat less easy to perform than writing a ballade. The Nobel Committee has yet to award any laurels to a woman simply for making her home a place of such peace and delight that her family might rightfully rise up and call her blessed—if such an odd notion ever occurred to them.

Nevertheless, ours is a true profession, ancient, honorable, and unique. Compared to it, all other careers are upstarts, Johnny-come-latelies. When physicians were barbers or even witch doctors, we were members in good standing of a guild already old. When bankers were usurers, lawyers no more than bardic historians, architects mere carpenters, writers simply minstrels, we existed much as we do today. We commanded the hearth, contrived the clothing, took charge of the children, flavored the food, and made the house—or the tent or the castle or the wattled hut or the cabin in the clearing—as attractive as our wits and our means permitted. When some early and talented woman patted her barley cake into a pleasanter shape than her neighbor's, or poured honey on it for a change from drippings, she was advancing her profession and, with it, civilization. When she complained that the floors were cold and persuaded her husband to let her use that extra bearskin for protection against drafts from the doorway, she was progressing another step along the route. It is true that most useful novelties, from the wheel to paper napkins and Scotch tape, have been conceived of first by men. But I suspect it was a housewife who fostered the notions to begin with.

"Really, dear, the children oughtn't to be sleeping on the floor," I can hear her saying to her man some winter night. "Why don't you invent a Bed?"

Or even, "Day in, day out, nothing but raw meat. I declare, I'm tired of it. Father, you're a clever fellow. How about discovering Fire?"

At our insistence have come most of the important amenities which cheer the lot of humankind—furniture, soap, Band-Aids, plumbing, chimneys, refrigerators, obstetrics, salt, dinner parties, and electric blendors. It is only while we are momentarily preoccupied with our current toys—while, as it were, our backs are turned—that men get into mischief and invent such useless gadgets as levers and catapults, airplanes and the hydrogen bomb.

It encourages me to remember that I belong to such an old and continuous company. I am pleased, also, as I said earlier, to remember how numberless are my fellow workers at this very moment. We have our illustrious ancestresses to boast of, like Nausicaa at the river's edge, rescuing Odysseus in the middle of the Monday wash, or Penelope busy at her loom in Ithaca. But we also have millions and millions of contemporary kin. That Indian woman, stirring her kettle of rice over a charcoal brazier, shares our responsibilities and our triumphs. So does her cousin in Hawaii or Nova Scotia, Kentucky or Kenya. In Alaskan igloos, in Swiss chalets and Spanish casas, in tenements, palaces, split-level ranch houses—every place in the world where men and children come home to sleep or eat or brag of their exploits or plan excursions or be comforted, housewives are concocting that comfort. We may be merely directing servants and altering flower arrangements. Or we may be weaving the very wool which goes into the family blankets. It is all one. On us rests the burden (and the glory) of seeing to it that the pot boils, the table is set, the sheets get changed, the babies remain healthy, a light shines in the window after dark, and there is refreshment for body and spirit waiting at the day's end.

Our tools change, of course. The besom gives way to the vacuum cleaner. We have carpets and linoleum in place of rushes or sand. Instead of the churn and the open-hearth spit, we have pressure cookers, thermostat-controlled ovens, and the milkman smiling at the door. The hired girl, willing and ubiquitous, has vanished; and that is no improvement. But at least we do now own a small army of electrical assistants. (Automation, for that matter, came to the household long before it really arrived in factories.) Still, the goals and the goods which it is our privilege to achieve on earth do not alter. They are the ones Naomi confided to Ruth, Joan worked toward for her Darby, and Eve undoubtedly understood.

All this being granted, one would think we should be constantly counting over our good fortune like beads. Our lineage noble, our aims important, we might seem to have little cause for discontent. Yet pride does not dwell in us as it should. The satisfaction I feel with my role is not universally shared. Doctors are, on the whole, happy to be doctors. Professors boast of their callings. Realtors lunch together and make complimentary speeches concerning their careers. But the housewives I encounter often go about with an injured air, complaining of their limitations rather than their benefits. The charges are diverse. But they seem to fall into three main catagories.

"We did not choose our profession," is the commonest of them. "It chose us."

If today were two or three hundred years ago, it might be a legitimate complaint. In other eras there *were* few other female careers. One could elect to remain unmarried, perhaps; but one was still bound by the chains of domesticity without even marital prestige to ease them. Or there was the cloister to run to. That was all. But nowadays women have as many occupations open to them as men and can be as selective in embracing them. We can be physicists or ambassadors, advertising experts or golf professionals. Doctor, lawyer, merchant, chief—name a career and it is within our reach. So when we choose to be housewives, we are only exercising free will. We enter that field with heads high and eyes open. Since so many of us do so choose—since the marriage rate is higher and the marriage age earlier and the children more numerous than they have been in a long while—the domestic arts appear, in the final summing-up, more appealing than we maintain. No, that particular accusation the defense cannot admit.

Less ordinary but more truthful is the charge that we grow up untrained for our duties, thrown without professional education into the most demanding of jobs. There the malcontents have a point. In other ages and times, girls were put to work from babyhood to learn the rudiments of their trade. While boys tramped off with older men to pick up the secrets of the chase or the caprices of war, while later they studied law or statecraft or were apprenticed to a guild master, girls were taken in hand by their mothers. They learned spinning and weaving, the mysteries of the kitchen, the nursery, the stillroom, and the ewery. Equality of education and expansion of opportunity changed all that. Boys began to get their professional training in colleges. Girls, busy with their books and their enlarged opportunities, began not getting it at all. In the present generation, and despite our largely servantless households, it is possible for them to spend twenty years or more learning to read, write, ski, translate Catullus, analyze minerals, run a typewriter, play chess or the guitar, sail a boat, or define Einstein's propositions, without ever having cooked a meal or run up a hem. Their mothers may be the most accomplished chatelaines in the neighborhood. But, "Girls are only young once," they comment to friends when a daughter drives off to Princeton for a weekend, leaving her room in chaos and her frocks unmended. "Time enough to be domestic when she has to be."

Happily enough, the girl in question often does learn to be domestic when she is confronted with that necessity. By osmosis, by environment, she has been indoctrinated in spite of herself with the elements of housewifery. She knows how a drawing room should look and an entrée taste. I have seen young women change before my eyes from slatterns scarcely competent to rinse out their lingerie while under the roof of childhood into perfectionists and *cordons bleus* in their own nests. It is not the easiest way to learn. It deprives our profession of its pomp. But trial, error, and simple goodwill can work miracles. So that argument fails also.

The third accusation is the most ancient one. It is a cry which has rung down through the years since first some long-haired skin-clad woman sulked in her cave, crossly blowing on the fire, and lamented that the hunters in the forest were having all the fun.

"Woman's work!" one hears like a threnody. "What is it but monotonous and frustrating and never finished? Three meals a day and a cart to push at the supermarket. A husband to please. Children to pick up after. Beds. Laundry. Pots and pans. All I have is this same dull round of chores forever asking to be done over again."

And the woman who complains, if she is especially tired or very bored, is apt to compare her lot with that of the man of the house.

"There he is in the city every day, mingling with grown-up people instead of the very young, having to please nobody except himself; taking two hours for lunch and dictating to a secretary and dreaming up notable deals. He hasn't any notion of what it means to be entirely surrounded by petty urgencies."

Does the charge have any validity? Well, some, of course, since all occupations have the defects of their virtues. Being a housewife is no sinecure. It means the plague of details all jobs entail. It implies frequent frustration, daily emergencies, sameness and routine, and not very much leisure. The average young woman married, say, ten years, by rights ought to sprout several hands to cope with all her problems. Let us say she has three children. (A few years ago it would have been one and a half. Now it is likelier, at least in our community, to be three, with a fourth on the way.) She has a cleaning woman once or twice a week. That is usually all the help she expects or can afford. She owns a washing machine and a dryer, an automatic dishwasher and fifty other recommended aids. But those do not order the groceries or buy the children's snowsuits or help them with their homework or feed the baby his spinach or scrub behind the cabinets. They merely permit her to keep abreast of her work. She needs stamina, cheerfulness, capability, and the forces of her whole being to cope with her position. But what, I wonder, has persuaded her that her husband's job took anything less from him?

A man's employment is not pure pleasure and recreation. If he is only a few years on his way to business success, he is still on the lower rungs of whatever ladder he has chosen to climb. He is his own man no more than his wife is her own woman. His bosses may be captious or his hirelings difficult. He has clients or patients or accounts or sponsors with all of whose crotchets he must bear. He has a living to earn and a family to succor, a house to support, a job to succeed or fail in. His days, exhilarating as they may sound to us housewives (left untidily at breakfast time with ten hours to cram full of ordinary tasks while he rushes away, well-tailored, to the office), are as disheveled as ours. A late or crowded train can be a greater frustration to a commuter than a stopped sink to us; and we, at least, can berate the plumber and so ventilate our spirits. He cannot argue with either the railroad or the head of the firm. We have neighbors to gossip with and confide in. We can even take a nap in the middle of the afternoon. He must be alert and agreeable at all times. It is tiring to clean a room. It is also fatiguing to compete in the marketplace. It is nerve-racking to have to answer the thousand questions of small children. It is more than nerve-racking, it is often ulcer-producing, to soothe the ruffled feathers of a whimsical employer.

That brisk and handsomely shaven junior executive on the station platform is as much at the mercy of occupational hazards as are we. Little annoyances will hinder him all day, too. A typist is inefficient. An order does not come through. An advertising campaign has not pleased the head of the company. His chief has a temper tantrum. The weather is bad, the car will not start, his pen runs out of ink, a memo is mislaid, he is rebuked by a customer, lunch is unappetizing. The difference between him and us lies in two things only: he is doing his job in a different atmosphere from the one where he sleeps and puts down roots, *and he has been trained from boyhood not to complain.* In other words, he has been taught the dignity of work. He is pleased to be a professional. If girls could be so trained and taught, perhaps the day-by-day vicissitudes of being a housewife, good at her trade, might seem less like the slings and arrows of outrageous fortune and more like simple obstacles to be overcome.

True, a man can change his job if he finds it altogether too trying to put up with. Or at least he can if he is bright, educated, successful, and lives in a prosperous era. And, true also, we are saddled with the selfsame duties pretty much for a lifetime. But then our difficult chores shrink faster than his. He will find time for leisure at a not much earlier age than sixty-five, and then sometimes too late to know enjoyment in it. We will have ten years of great effort; if the family is large, perhaps twenty. After that we will have more hours on our hands than some of us will know what to do with. The children will be in school or even away from home altogether. Drudgeries will dwindle. We'll have time for any avocation to which our gifts entitle us. We'll be free to paint, write, garden, run for Congress, chair the Woman's Club, talk from soapboxes, change the color of our hair, do good works, take up petit point, read good books, or start a business.

And in the meantime—during the course of those ten or twenty difficult and demanding years—we will have won rewards out of all proportion to his even if we did not recognize them as rewards at the moment.

From the raw material of four walls and a roof, a shelter over our heads, we will have made a home by force of our own personalities. We will have warmed, cheered, and sustained the head of that house, turned progeny into a family. We will have learned a dozen skills and enjoyed the fruits of such skills. For us the baby will have taken his first step, repeated his first word. We will have heard the schoolchild call "Mommy" as soon as he puts a foot inside the door, not so much to have a reply as to be assured that he is safe, life is ordinary, and that *We* are there. We will have been raised to a dizzy eminence as final authority, dispenser of justice, necessary Presence. A husband, no matter how willingly he gives himself to the role of householder or parent, never approaches such triumphs. To be jealous of his public busyness, then—which is at the core of the complaint—is to denigrate ourselves and our worth.

In reality, all the stock reproaches fail when they are logically examined, this one most of all.

Free choice, importance, the prizes as well as the perils of a career—they are all ours. What more can one ask of a profession? And the fact that we belong to the most ancient of any is, at least for me, the crowning feather in an enviable and becoming cap. God, as I said when I began, must love housewives. It is time we also learned to love ourselves.

3 *A Jewel in the Pocket*

There is this to be said for the lot of the housewife—it is not an obscure calling. These days we are News. Not since high-flying Icarus sailed too near the sun, melting off his wax wings and so setting the science of aviation back several thousand years, has so much discussion gone on about a single profession.

Radio panels debate our position in the world, television sponsors whistle for our attention. Advertising campaigns are planned with us in mind. Psychologists analyze our motives. Foundations examine our needs and industry gears its output to their findings. Ashley Montagu admires us (at least as women), while Margaret Mead accuses us of escaping from our civic responsibilities into the warm nest of "fecundity." We are praised, abused, consulted, quoted, advised. We are seldom ignored.

The latest group to turn the microscope upon us for its own purposes is the colleges. And the colleges—especially the women's colleges—are very cross with us indeed. They say we are misusing our opportunities. They charge us with betraying our education. The argument runs something like this:

Four years at a good university or college is an expensive proposition for both the student and the institution. Although placement in such schools is growing steadily more competitive, a larger and larger percent of American girls are now either studying there or readying themselves to apply. Once enrolled they will—if they are to keep up with curricular demands—work hard, learn much, come out educated and informed young women. Yet what, ask the critics, happens to most of them? They either marry immediately or else work for a year or two and *then* marry, tossing their skills and talents onto the domestic scrap heap. All that hard-got gold of knowledge will waste unused. Or, to change the figure slightly, that many-faceted jewel will be popped carelessly into the pocket of a kitchen apron, there to slither about with the small change of daily living until it tarnishes or is lost.

The young scientist will not proceed with science. The Greek major will no longer parse Euripides. Government will get scant help from promising history specialists. Students of everything from archaeology and art to zoology will settle down into the suburban or the urban round, with their skills rusting, their minds deteriorating, their capabilities withering away.

One educator has gone so far as to submit a stern plan. She formidably argues that a college girl should be forced to sign a pledge with the college before she gets her diploma, promising a certain number of years of professional work to be paid, seemingly, to industry or the state, like conscience money, after she graduates. No job, no degree. Thus the girl will be put on terms of equality with the young man forced to do his military service before he dares relapse into civilian life. It is a Spartan scheme with all sorts of horrid totalitarian overtones. One has only to recall what happened to Sparta to reject that bit of iron nonsense.

Dr. Bunting of Radcliffe has made a more sensible suggestion. In fact, she has gone beyond suggestion and invented a full-blown working arrangement. Women who have been away for a while from the academic world can now return to Radcliffe as fellows or researchers, to teach, study, write, paint, or discover a new star in the galaxy. They are housed and subsidized, and so coaxed back into nondomestic usefulness. Here is a commendable idea and one which will benefit both colleges and housewives emeritus.

It will benefit the latter, that is to say, so long as it does not unsettle them before their time. For what is wrong with the first plan and suspect about the second is the limited, utilitarian approach, a kind of philosophical myopia. They imply two erroneous beliefs: first, that being a housewife is not a noble, useful, and rewarding career; and, second, that education has no value unless it is brought to the marketplace.

The first proposition is a holdover from the feminist movement which enchanted our grandmothers and great-grandmothers. They fought real battles and helped abolish real injustices. They won, for women, working freedom, equality of educational opportunity, and the vote. But a crusader has always to cling fiercely to one side of an argument only, or lose her fire. The old warriors who fought in those skirmishes lost sight deliberately of the pleasure and gratifications of domesticity per se, which we have rediscovered. They instilled in their descendants a sort of Puritan thrust, the feeling that a woman has no right to be anything less than a public citizen.

"Females of the world, unite!" was emblazoned on their banners. "You have nothing to lose but your chains."

Unfortunately, by chains they meant the demands of kitchen, nursery, the home.

We are their heirs even though we have half forgotten the frame of mind which induced such thinking. In our generation we have been able to stop battling for public rights and relapse into household life with relief, much as a dolphin, escaped from the net, gratefully leaps back into the natural sea. But the doctrines they fought for still unconsciously plague us. As even an atheist is haunted by a sense of original sin, we emancipated housewives of this century are beset by a feeling of guilt if we simply stay home and mind the hearth. To bring up a family is not enough. To keep house, assist the schools, become Gray Ladies in hospitals—to cosset a husband, take our children to orthodontists, embellish a garden, attend concerts, entertain our friends—is insufficient. We must somehow impress our personalities and our accomplishments on the outside world.

"I was head of my class in English literature," one laments. "Now I have scarcely time to open a book. Is it wrong of me to stay so involved with the house and the children?"

Or, "What use was my education? Four years of college and a magna cum laude degree—and I've never earned a penny of my own. It seems such a waste."

They will go on believing it a waste so long as they are told so by those they think of as their betters.

Do not misunderstand me. I have nothing at all against housewives who use their education and their brains outside the home. I have, from time to time, used mine. The affairs of the world might come grindingly to a halt if women did not serve that world. Let housewives, if they have energy and ability, be domestic "moonlighters." By all means encourage them to write books, run factories, direct traffic, play the stock market, give to the poor, assist the League of Women Voters, design machines, or decorate other people's houses, if it gives them pleasure or enhances their lives. I will even agree that nurses, doctors, engineers, and lawyers who clamor for admittance to overcrowded professional schools should somehow manage to put their training to use. There is a real shortage of such colleges and a real need for such talents. When girls undertake that training they may be elbowing aside some man who would eventually better return society's investment. How they are to work out the debt, I do not know. It is a problem for the colleges, society itself, and their consciences. Perhaps in such fields, Dr. Bunting's plan would be particularly profitable. After women had reared their families, they might well return to the courts, the hospitals, the factories and put their skills to work.

What I do object to is the charge that a liberal arts education is on a level with technical training—that college women are guilty of a misdemeanor when they are employed only in the home. I do not like to see our profession so assailed or its adherents made to feel ashamed of their vocations.

Particularly, I resent seeing education held so cheap.

It is that second proposition which seems to me subversive—the heresy that knowledge has no value unless it can be measured against earning power or public works.

For a liberal arts education is not a tool like a hoe or a blueprint or an electric mixer. It is a true and precious stone which can glow just as wholesomely on a kitchen table as when it is put on exhibition in a jeweler's window or bartered for bread and butter. Learning is a boon, a personal good. It is a light in the mind, a pleasure for the spirit, an object to be enjoyed. It is refreshment, warmth, illumination, a window from which we get a view of the world. To what barbarian plane are we descending when we demand that it serve only the economy? And how has the world progressed if that very female education which was so bravely demanded for a hundred years is to be denied to the people it was meant to benefit?

Four centuries ago there lived in England a man named Sir Thomas More, who was that nation's most just judge, greatest Chancellor, and liveliest conscience. He was a reformer, believing that knowledge, next to virtue, was the most desirable thing in life. He also held the iconoclastic notion that women were intellectually as capable as men. So in spite of the prevailing patterns of his day, he gave to his daughters the same education he gave his son. He taught them Greek, Latin, logic, philosophy, mathematics, and astronomy. Certainly he had no expectation that Margaret or Cecily or Elizabeth would become a classics professor or a clerk or accountant. He just hoped they would be fortunate and happy wives. He wanted them to be able to wear learning like a bracelet on the arm or a diamond at the throat. They had as much right to the jewel, he felt, as men. There were critics in his day (among them, Henry VIII) who rather thought the girls were wasting their time. What good were such accomplishments to young women who would spend most of their adult lives rearing children and supervising the making of puddings and cheese?

But, "What a delight is truth!" said More. And he went on making Latin puns for Margaret's amusement and discussing Livy with Cecily as calmly as he later lost his head for a principle.

It is an ironic commentary on this century that we have sloughed off the social abuses of the sixteenth, yet retain its sense of educational values—or, rather, have lowered those values. For men of that time genuinely cherished the arts as adornments. If their chief professions were statecraft, war, and theology, learning was their recreation. It should be ours today, with the vital difference that it ought to be the recreation of two sexes instead of one.

To assert that housewives have no right to the simple joys of knowing is to denigrate everything best in civilization. Are we going back to the medieval thesis that education unfits a woman to change a diaper or make a lemon meringue pie? Are we to believe that because a girl has studied the pre-Stuart dramatists she will be less well equipped than her uneducated sister to prod a grapefruit at the grocer's or scour a sink? Or are we, on the other hand, to give credence to the idea that prodding grapefruit and scouring sinks are unworthy occupations for an educated human being? Both notions seem to me the wildest sort of reaction.

Surely the ability to enjoy Heine's exquisite melancholy in the original German will not cripple a girl's talent for making chocolate brownies. Nor will the fact that she likes to read a cookbook keep her from taking pleasure in rereading Keats. Provided she has not been taught that cooking and using a vacuum sweeper are degrading, each talent will supplement the other. She will be able to judge a newspaper item more sensibly, understand a politician's speech more sagely, talk over her husband's business problems with him more helpfully, and entertain her children more amusingly if her brain is tuned and humming with knowledge. Perhaps Plato will turn out to be as useful to her as Dr. Spock, and Chaucer wiser than a marriage counselor. To have written a senior thesis on the frescoes of Giotto may seem at first glance no practical training for someone who will put in most of the succeeding fifteen or twenty years feeding sandwiches to cub scouts or driving little girls to dancing class. Yet in what way is it a waste? The glories of Renaissance Art will still be there in her consciousness, ready to entertain her when television palls. An acquaintanceship with global geography might extend her awareness of world problems and make her a more useful citizen. Knowing how to translate Proust might improve, say, her cooking; and botany sharpen her gardening abilities. I don't say they would. They might.

But if those attainments never in all her years as a housewife proved to have the slightest practical or marketable application, they would be still dear and valuable. They would add another dimension, an extra richness to existence.

When I was a freshman at college in California,. I took a course called "Latin-American History." It was taught by an inspired and passionate man who loved his subject. Because of his eloquence, I have forgotten scarcely a date or an episode from that chronicle of adventure. The feats of Pizarro's tiny band, overcoming half a continent with a vest-pocket army as greedy as it was gallant; the romantic story of the Inca emperor who fell in love with his conquered princess and so brought about the division of his kingdom and its destruction; the fate of Atahualpa, son of that love affair, who believed the Spanish promises—they all live in my mind as they did years ago. Although my spelling is generally so erratic that I am likely to put two *c*'s in *necessity* if nobody nudges me, I can still write out their exotic names correctly.

That knowledge has never been of the slightest assistance to me in either earning a living or keeping my house. I don't even get around to using it for dazzling my dinner partner at a party. "Read any good books lately about the conquest of Peru?" is hardly the sort of gambit to assure the success of an evening, when what the man on my right wants to talk about is his golf score.

But I would not part with that portion of my education for half my own kingdom. I am grateful for such fragments as still float about in my imagination. They are part of my dowry, as precious to me as my grandmother's silver spoons, and as ready to be passed on to my descendants if they want them. I wish I owned a larger inheritance. I wish I could read Greek and knew more about Physics and could understand the Latin footnotes in scholarly books. I do not want to teach those things to other people, particularly, or brandish them like weapons or use them to earn my bread. I just like to have a well-furnished mind.

Housewives more than any other race deserve well-furnished minds. They have to live in them such a lot of the time. To say that our education must be functional—that we must put it to practical use or not accept it—is as silly as to deny us the right to buy antiques for our parlors or silver and crystal for our tables when stainless steel forks and Grand Rapids chairs would serve us just as well in the long run.

Young men emerging from *their* colleges with liberal arts degrees are not expected to use in their jobs all the things they learned at Yale or Brown or the University of Arizona. The advertising executive may find that his knowledge of romantic poetry in the Nineteenth Century does not help him present a campaign to a sponsor. The lawyer drawing up a deed is not practically benefited by having once, perhaps, studied Xenophon. Understanding calculus will be of no particular importance to the boy who takes over his father's automobile agency. But no one charges that those young men are betraying their educations. So far as I can determine, the heads of men's colleges are not worried about imparting a mass of unfunctional classical facts to their undergraduates. In fact, the drive is all in the other direction. Industrial management begs for applicants with a solid knowledge of the humanities. Medical schools ask for candidates educated in something besides science. Law schools implore beginners to bring with them a command of English syntax.

Surely the profession of housewife deserves as well from society. We who belong to that profession hold the fate of the world in our hands. It is our influence which will determine the culture of coming generations. We are the people who chiefly listen to the music, buy the books, attend the theater, prowl the art galleries, collect for the charities, brood over the schools, converse with the children. Our minds need to be rich and flexible for those duties.

And even if we had no such duties, we could still honorably wear our education as the ornament it is, with no other excuse than that it becomes us. Or if we prefer to keep it in an apron pocket to finger like an amulet, that is also our right. The jewel need not wear out or lose its value or grow dull there, so long as we understand its worth. It is something we have earned by our own efforts. And not even the clamor of household voices or the complaints of a fulminating college dean can destroy for us our joy in its possession.

4 ❧ *How Not to Kill Your Husband*

Talk all you like about automatic ovens and electric lishwashers, there is nothing you can have around the iouse so useful as a husband.

Besides being so efficient as a breadwinner, he owns a iost of other amiable talents. He takes care of luggage on ourneys. He carries out the trash cans of evening. He nakes a handy parent, and he is extraordinarily good at ipping one's dresses up the back. Keeping him happy and xtant would seem of the most urgent self-interest to any ensible, affectionate housewife.

Yet women are being constantly accused these days of illing off our spouses prematurely. Men die young and ve are to blame, say the researchers. We harass our man nto ulcers. We set up as his rival and give him heart atacks. We either overfeed him into obesity or starve him vith a diet of thawed-out dinners. We are at once domieering and helpless, a dragging anchor or a cruel goad; mbitious, ambivalent, a mess.

We who read the books or assimilate the lectures have lmost begun to wonder if the critics may not be right. Vhat *have* we done to men that they should seem so eculiarly fragile and vulnerable in this century? It is perfectly true that we persistently outlive them. Old cemeteries bristle with headstones inscribed to patriarchs of another era who buried three wives and flourished into their eighties or nineties, vigorous, optimistic, and tyrannical. Now, scanning statistics, we shudder at an opposite phenomenon, a prevalence of widows. Forgetting that vitamins and the science of obstetrics have simply permitted the tougher sex—ours—to live out our allotted span at last, we begin to feel guilty as Eve. We whirl like dervishes, listening to all voices and trying to obey all oracles. We pack the children off to bed early so our man will find, when he returns from work, a quiet house and a wife willing to hear his troubles. We take an intelligent interest in his business, entertain his clients, drive his car for him, keep from him the frustrations of our own day. We come down, tidy to the last curl, to give him a proper, conversational breakfast in the mornings. With all our might, we blow on the embers of romance, trying at the same time to be the bride he married and the helpmate we promised to become.

I have an idea we are trying too hard. Self-consciousness can mutilate marriage. If women are to reinstate men as the long-lived gender, perhaps what we ought to be guided by is expedience and common sense.

We might, maybe, take a leaf from modern pediatricians who preach a doctrine new in the last twenty years. There was a time previous to that when doctors treated mothers like imbeciles. We weren't allowed to pick up our progeny when they cried or feed them except at iron intervals. The nursery was run like a regimented camp and mothers were turned into unwilling jailers. When it was discovered that children under that formal treatment grew up just as neurotic, frail, and maladjusted as before, everything changed. We are now urged to dandle Junior if he seems unhappy, spank him when he is unbearable, and feed him on demand.

"Know your own child," urges the new gospel. "Study him rather than the books."

Who knows? The self-winding plan might work for husbands, too. Every marriage is an individual combination of forces; every man, every woman is unique. Kindness may kill one husband, unconcern another. The hermitage of home is what a certain sort of nature needs; gregarious men might pine away without company several times a week. It is the needs of the singular creature we live with which we must study.

Or better still, why not let him decide what agrees with him? A determined baby can bring up his mother quite nicely when he puts his mind to it. Husbands are surely as bright as babies. Left to themselves, they might work out acceptable schemes for their proper feeding and care, and educate their wives accordingly.

I know one household where that system operates successfully. Ours.

Of course, I must admit my husband is a man with a lively sense of survival. He understood my limitations and his own, and from the start he determined how to cope with both. I'm not sure it was a conscious coping. He just took me good-naturedly by the hand and hurried me along a path that seemed suitable to him.

That path might not look alluring to everyone, and I do not urge our technique on others. In the first place, I'm against advice. In the second place, any advice I gave would sound pretty silly. When my marriageable granddaughters (if I am lucky enough to have any) cluster at my knee, begging me to tell them how I managed to preserve Grandfather into hale and mischievous old age, they are bound to raise their eyebrows as I respond dreamily, "Well, we never ate breakfast together."

Yet never eating breakfast together is the simple cornerstone of our marriage and my husband's bounding good health. It has not been an easy rule to keep. Having been strictly brought up, I knew how every man should be sent off to work—heartily fed, heartened by soothing conversation, waved farewell to at the door.

The trouble is that I am a late starter, my husband an early one. He leaps out of bed at morning, caroling, "What a beautiful day!" before he has so much as looked out of the window. I won't even admit it *is* morning, and wish it would go away. I like to fortify myself with eggs and bacon or something childish like last night's leftover cupcakes. He wants two large cups of tepid coffee (it's faster to swallow than hot coffee) and exactly three slices of lukewarm toast. To him at break of day, time is more important than food. He actually enjoys hurrying as other men enjoy a good game of tennis, and to sit down to a leisurely morning meal would kill his spirit. Thirty minutes is the most he allows himself for shaving, showering, dressing, bolting his calories, driving his ritual mile and a half, and swinging aboard the last car of the commuting train just as it pulls out of the station. A lesser man might die of the practice. That race merely quickens his blood, strengthens his muscle, and keeps his arteries in condition.

After our first few stunned matutinal encounters, with

me blundering blindly about the kitchen trying to interest him in an omelet—an endeavor somewhat like trying to deflect an Atlas missile—we came to an agreement.

"Look, pet," he said firmly on the fourth morning, "stop acting like the Ideal Wife in a soap opera. I don't *want* a domestic scene before eight A.M. I'll promise not to strike you with a blunt instrument if you'll promise not to lift that little tousled head off the pillow till I get out the back door."

So for more years than I care to count, I have laid his place the night before, left a loaf near the toaster, and allowed his coffee to be barbarically heated over by himself.

It still goes against my housewifely grain. But to this amicable arrangement I credit the fact that his doctor annually congratulates him on his beautiful blood pressure.

He has never been able to claim the status symbol of an ulcer, either. And perhaps this is because, with complete disregard for expert counsel, he has trained me to take no interest, intelligent or otherwise, in his work. I mean the work which earns us our living. The office to him is the office. Home is home. He doesn't want the two confused. I know his address, I know his secretary by name and voice, and I know exactly how flexible is our budget. But I learned fairly quickly that greeting him at the station with a glad cry of, "Darling! How did things go today?" and urging him at dinner to "explain all over again how you worked out that problem in employee relations" are undesirable gambits. What he wants to talk about in the evening is the progress of the rose bed or the gossip of the neighbors or the books we are both reading or what our daughters are currently up to.

And he wants to talk about it promptly. At the table, fifteen minutes after he gets inside the door. Not for him the twilight interval suggested by romantic columnists, that hour before dinner when a wife is supposed to dispense with the children, slip into something soft and loose, and console her husband for the day's defeats. My husband admits to no defeats. He can do his own relaxing at his own pace. Lounging before a wood fire with a pitcher of martinis at his elbow is not his idea of a seven o'clock treat. He wants his dinner—and no wonder, with the breakfast he eats. He wants to slip into something loose, himself, and sit down at once to large helpings of hearty food, topped off by a rich homemade dessert. Then if it is winter, he wants to refinish a piece of furniture in the basement or play half an hour of swing music on the piano or watch a bit of television. If it is summer, he wishes to walk grandly about our half-acre, addressing each flower by name and admonishing the lawn to grow. When the children were younger and at home, he wanted them tagging at his heels, noisy and intrusive, instead of tucked submissively into bed. His regimen might give nightmares to marriage counselors and life-expectancy experts. It is his definition of how to live longer and like it.

No, he doesn't want to tell me his troubles. Eccentrically, he prefers to hear about mine, particularly if they have something to do with the furnace or a short circuit. I felt a terrible failure the first time I met him at evening with a wail of, "The sink! It's stopped up and I can't reach a plumber."

The shades of all my ancestresses reproached me. But I had underestimated him. He is an incorrigible handyman, one who finds a plumbing problem engrossing as chess. (He likes chess, too.) His eyes lit up, he darted down to the basement, fiddled with a pipe or two, and in half an hour all was well with the drains. And he was as triumphant, as willing to be complimented, as if he had just reported pulling off a merger. Nothing makes him happier than a long list of small crises to which he can attend on Saturdays. Nothing keeps him fitter than an evening spent peering into the bowels of the fuse box or tinkering with a recalcitrant faucet. What does dangerously raise his temperature is for me to call a professional artisan without first asking his permission.

Once, on his birthday, I gave him an air conditioner as a surprise. I did not consult him; just had it installed in his study, where I thought he could find respite from August heat if a briefcase demanded his attention. He was polite. He professed a hypocritical pleasure. But he never used the thing. Later, he confessed he hated all air conditioners, but I don't believe it for a minute, since he has never complained of the one which cools his office. His dignity had been outraged by my actually buying a household gadget which he had not personally shopped for, designed, or inspected. I have never again committed a similar crime.

The fact that I am by nature a mechanical moron scarcely enters into this. I'm trainable. Given a different husband, one who didn't know an angle iron from a plumber's friend, I might have gone on to fairly glorious heights. I might have learned to fill my own fountain pen or been able to work the trip mechanism on the washing machine. Still, as I say, we have this arrangement and it pleases us both.

"But, Granny," I can hear my young questioners protest, "surely you must have done something positive. What about difficult things like persuading him out of bad bachelor habits? What about remembering not to nag?"

"Oh," I shall admit, "you have a point there. I *was* creative about his habits. I worked on his and he worked on mine. If I was inclined to be prompt to the pitch of obsession—the kind of person who sits twenty minutes in an empty station for fear the train may somehow be ahead of schedule—he was cavalier about time. He drank coffee to excess and I liked to stay up late without it. I was economical, he insouciant about expenses. I forgot to turn out lights and he put off writing letters. Little things like that.

"And you know what? We reformed each other. We both began to be dilatory together. We both learned to buy something we could not afford when we were feeling most insolvent, as a lift to morale. Together we read until the small hours, drank coffee just before bedtime, left lamps burning in all the rooms, and forgot about part of our correspondence. It was wonderful how friction vanished once we had enough faults in common."

But as for nagging (I shall have to own), of course I nagged. I do to this day. What wife worth her salt isn't a scold by inclination and necessity? I nag him to buy new sports jackets for himself instead of gifts for me, into getting a reasonable amount of sleep, into letting the storm windows go when something pleasanter offers itself. I nag him about earning more money, too—I say it isn't necessary. Any moment, now, I'm going to nag him into retiring years before the mandatory age so he can settle down to the serious gardening or the frivolous music which are his real vocations.

Other wives, other methods.

"Let him educate you," I shall tell those still-imaginary girls. "The whole duty of a wife is to bolster her husband's self-esteem; not his vanity but his pride. A man's ego bruises easily. It is not nourished like a woman's by the sheer biological ability to bear children.

"Besides," I shall insist, "women can learn such a lot from men. They own by instinct certain simple masculine virtues we ought to imitate."

My own generous instructor took pains with my lessons. He taught me enthusiasm and what I know of tact and how to give in gracefully when one *has* to give in.

"Never grant a favor grudgingly," he warned me a long time ago. "If you are going to grant it anyway, do it wholeheartedly. Otherwise it's not a favor."

That bit of dogma has been of great use to me in dealing with children, committees, and domestic help. It has also saved me on occasion from wrapping myself up in an unbecoming cloak of self-righteousness. It's all very well to abandon one's idea of a luxurious Caribbean cruise because one's husband prefers a picturesque holiday in the cold Maine woods. But what good is that holiday to him if his companion keeps him aware of her magnanimity all the while he is trying to land a trout or light a fire in the cabin?

He has taught me to keep my chin up in a bleak season, and the thermostat down. From him I have learned the difference between a flicker and a freckled thrush, how to appreciate the esthetics of baseball, and the way to treat a man who is coming down with a cold. (Walk softly and carry your own storm shelter.)

He has impressed on me the importance of thanking him as prettily when he takes me out to dinner as I would a stranger who had done me a service. In fact he has drilled me ceaselessly in the uses of praise. *He* doesn't wait for me to summon up a compliment when one is required. He cheerfully demands it. For a promotion or a triumph in seeding tuberous-rooted begonias, for a present he has brought me, or for a glimpse of his fortnightly haircut—he cues me just when to come in with appropriate murmurs of admiration. Praise is better than wheat germ for even the least vain of men, and every wife ought to keep a supply in her pocket ready to scatter like manna. Perhaps it is because I have studied that lesson carefully that he still fits into his college dinner jacket and believes he has insomnia if he has to take more than three deep breaths at night before he falls asleep.

"But you learned nothing on your own?" the girls may ask with disappointment.

"I had one original virtue," I shall say proudly. "I was a Perfect Passenger."

There are wives who know more about driving a car than a whole ambulance corps and still their husbands thrive. Mine would pine away if I insisted on being co-chauffeur. He is a born navigator, jealous of the wheel, inclining to tell New York City taxi drivers how to duck the traffic on Third Avenue and suffering audibly if he is forced into the back seat of any moving vehicle. Aboard a plane, I am always surprised he doesn't go forward and ask to take over the controls. In me he found a woman to his specifications. I can drive, but I don't particularly want to, much preferring to peer thoughtfully at the passing scenery. I don't point out shortcuts because I don't notice them. Since I have no compulsion to brake, steer, or comment on our speed, motor journeys for us are always occasions of mutual enjoyment.

I have ridden with couples who found them otherwise.

We were once driving with friends on a Connecticut throughway, with no one in the car quite sure of the route. Suddenly the wife, on most occasions a diplomatic woman, gave a shriek of warning.

"There!" she commanded. "Off to the right. That's our road."

"Dammit," her husband muttered through his teeth, as he drove straight past the directional signs and onto a long lane which had practically no turning before Boston, "why did you have to tell me? It's where I was *going*."

In our life together my husband and I have had disagreements but none concerning an automobile. And both the vehicular-insurance people and his physician consider him a very good risk still.

Axioms like that I shall be glad to pass on to my descendants. I shall tell them how I've never been quite sure whether or not marriage is a partnership as people claim, but I'm quite sure it is not a tug-of-war. What most barbarously frays the marital rope is two natures pulling two opposite ways. I shall explain to them how hard on a man's health are the sulks and pouts and reconciliations of the honeymoon—that three months is long enough for any girl to remain a bride. I shall give them all my best recipes along with my silver spoons and insist they let their husbands worry about their own waistlines. I shall suggest that winning the last word is a dubious victory.

But one axiom, and the most important, I shall keep to myself. For why should I bother advising any young wife about feeding her man on a diet of pure affection? It is true that husbands, like babies and other people, thrive on love and wither without it. It is the best life-preserving medicine in existence. But any woman who can't figure that out for herself will never learn it anyhow.

5 ✤ *The Moonlight Adventure*

The Post Office Department, I see by the papers, is having trouble making ends meet financially. It doesn't surprise me. My morning mail, which comes these days in the afternoon (for the route is long and our postman a conversationalist), is full of messages I don't really want to read. There are the eternal throwaways addressed anonymously to "Occupant" which I toss unopened into the wastebasket. There are the advertisements for a new detergent, or for something with a bellicose four-letter name like "Slay," threatening to assassinate the crabgrass we cherish because at least it's green. My congressman urges me to support the party. The Home for Indigent Widows of Deceased Bird Watchers solicits my contribution. And there is one constantly recurring letter, the gist of which I can now repeat in my sleep.

> *Dear Miss McGinley* [it says; or sometimes, *Dear Miss McGill* or *Miss McGiniss* or even *McGinkley*]:
> *Will you appear the first Friday in March on a panel arranged by our club to discuss the question "Do Housewives Have a Right to Hold Jobs after Marriage?"*

The request flatters me even while I understand how numerous are the clubs of America and how short the supply of unpaid speakers. (When I was a member in good standing of the PTA, I used to have to try myself to persuade reluctant authors to give tongue.) Although I know my own limitations and never accept the challenge, I am touched that some respected organization, however misguidedly, pines to hear my voice upraised in argument. Still, I am puzzled by the question provided for the debate.

"Should housewives work after marriage?" is an excessively innocent query. It implies that jobs and housewives have scarcely met, that wives-and-mothers are just now timidly peering out the door to test a public wind. Is there, it seems to ask, any place for them in the great world?

With women representing more than 40 percent of the nation's labor force, and with so large a proportion of those women married, it is hard to see what remains to discuss. The working housewife, the "moonlighter" doing two jobs, is not an academic question but a fact of modern life. She is the pretty secretary in the office, seeing her husband through medical school. She is the teacher, the social worker, the librarian, the fashion designer. She works in factories, supermarkets, laboratories; sells antiques, assists the dentist, clerks in department stores, writes copy in advertising agencies. She is the diplomat, the scientist, the architect, the historian, the corporation head. She is also the weekly char. She is not even a modern phenomenon, for there have always been wives who helped their husbands in the shop, or farm women who kept hens and brought the eggs to market on Saturdays.

The new question, the one which agitates sociologists

and feminists these latter days, seems to be the opposite topic: Do housewives have a right *not* to work after marriage? The same people who berate us for keeping our education in the pocket of a kitchen apron also scold us for clinging to the hearth as our sole profession. Given these recent freedoms of ours, including the liberty to compete with men on nearly equal terms, we are traitors to our class, they tell us, if we merely relapse into the role which confined us for so many thousands of years.

On this point I do have opinions, firm if unorthodox by the new gospel, the Word which preaches fulfillment of the individual ego. Women, I insist, have more than a right to remain housewives if they like. In ordinary circumstances, and given ordinary gifts, they own almost a mandate. So highly do I regard our profession and its importance to the human scheme, it seems to me occupation sufficient to fill a life, a heart. In an ideal society we would want no other work. Men would earn the bread, we would bring up the family. We would unsettle no masculine pride by competition in masculine fields, divert none of the male energy from its proper preoccupation with the business and discoveries of the public world. The two nations, male and female, would each inhabit a sphere snugly suited to its ordained capabilities. The hunter, man, could range as widely as he pleased, sustained and supported by the shielded fire at home. Women would slice the loaf, draw the curtains, care for the children, dispense charity, patronize and perhaps create the fine arts. But this is not an ideal society or a perfect world. Nor are human beings neat little pegs arranged in orderly rows of fitted slots.

There are a hundred reasons why women must and should continue to undertake the moonlight adventure.

The commonest involves money. It always has. Salaries and household budgets are not automatically compatible. The young marry earlier than they did, before the husband is established in business, before he has a house to which to bring his bride. He may not have finished his education. It is a rare young woman these days who does not, for a while, go on with whatever job has involved her before marriage. In most such situations, the outcome is self-resolving. The husband is promoted. A baby arrives. Or the pair simply learn to live on one income and make do.

Sometimes, though, money continues to be needed for emergencies—for taking care of an elderly parent or the children's education or the bill of the orthodontist. Perhaps there has been a business failure or a loss of salary. The housewife, as she has been doing since the beginning of the universe, ungrudgingly takes on the burden of winning a little extra bread.

Those are the ordinary cases, and they cause little inconvenience to anyone except the moonlighter herself. She is not vying with her husband, only assisting him. Somehow she manages, with the strength of the driven, to continue with her outside work and at the same time assemble meals, keep the house clean, get the children off to school, and comfort them at bedtime. It may not be the best way of bringing up a family or channeling her emotional thrust, but it can be done. Often the children in such a family grow up more self-reliant and appreciative than those with a full-time, indulgent mother.

It is when the job becomes more important to her than

the household, or when the extra money it brings in becomes too tempting in itself, that tensions arise. This is not only an affluent society, it is a greedy one. New cars, wall-to-wall carpeting, steak for the table, dishwashers, and barbecue pits—those are the curious goals which sometimes entice women away from home into factories and offices; and they do not seem to me satisfactory ones. Women fulfill themselves best when they give themselves away. To go to business because the children need a summer camp or must have their teeth straightened is a perfectly adequate motive. To moonlight because the neighbor's new kitchen is outshining hers, and her wages will pay for an oven built into the wall, is avarice. And even though the working housewife has energy to spare, even if she does not lacerate her husband's self-esteem by refusing to rely on him, such efforts are often uneconomic. It costs money to work. Lunches and a wardrobe and paid help for the house eat up a women's earnings. It is ironic, in fact, that at a time when women have opportunity and the world's blessing to be careerists of any sort they choose, the supply of household servants dwindles almost to the vanishing point. Perhaps it is an appropriate way of keeping the mortal balance, and women out of the labor market.

I once talked to the wife of a professor who was herself a college teacher.

"When the children were little," she told me, "I spent a good deal more than I made. My salary was small. I couldn't keep track of the food budget properly. And in order to get competent nurses and cleaning help, I had to lay out an astronomic sum."

"Then why did you bother?" I asked her.

"Because if I didn't continue teaching then, I could never have got back to it later on. What is more, my husband almost demanded that I go on with it. He thought I had talent. And he felt we would both be happier if I was doing something I enjoyed more than housekeeping."

It is such cases as hers which are exceptional enough to maintain the rule. For while I believe that women should never feel ashamed for preferring to cleave to the domestic career, I also believe they ought to have a choice of vocations.

Some women may be unfitted by temperament for the daily round of household chores. They may be affectionate wives, loving mothers; they merely detest mending and shopping for groceries and counting out laundry and drinking coffee with neighbors—all tasks the rest of us absentmindedly enjoy. If they have public abilities, if they have health, stamina, opportunity, it is possible that everybody concerned will be better off when they work outside the home. They will tell a happier bedtime story if they have not had to entertain the children all day. They will be kinder to their husbands, more even-tempered to their progeny, more efficient as women. Weekends will seem to them vacations, not ordeals.

I know a woman who after some years of being cook, nursemaid, and nervous wreck returned to the newspaper where she had been a minor luminary before she married. She now looks five years younger, her children are no longer problems, and her husband has stopped taking too many cocktails before dinner.

I also know a Horrible Example. This woman, before marriage, had managed to get one high-instepped foot on the first rung of the publishing ladder. She was an associate editor of an important magazine. Her husband was a law student, and she continued to make herself useful and respected at work while he finished college and cast about for a practice.

At the end of five or six years she was an outstanding success, almost a celebrity in her field—highly paid, useful. Her vitality, mental and physical, was enormous. But she was a systematic creature, a conscientious wife. And she had certain social ambitions. In her mind she carried an image of the ideal family. The proper thing to do at a certain stage of marriage, she felt, was to leave business, have a couple of children, and assemble her life around them. Unfortunately, she had underestimated her own drive and need for power. All the executive energy she had spent on the magazine under her care (actually she could have operated a factory or commanded an army with equal ease) she channeled into running her household. She pushed her husband up *his* ladder until he had a heart attack at forty-four. Her three children—who would have been only two if the boy had not delayed his arrival until there were already a pair of sisters—were chivvied and pruned and tugged at and sent to the right schools and pushed into the correct dancing classes and relentlessly arranged until they turned into spiritless robots.

Now, in her early fifties, she has exhausted her own resources. There are yet no grandchildren to occupy her. She is chairman of half a dozen clubs but they do not satisfy her. She plans charity balls but her heart is not in it. She is unhappy. *There* is a woman who should never have stopped moonlighting. Doing two jobs and doing them magnificently would have been child's play to her; she would have made a contribution to both publishing and her family. And the victims of her good intentions would have been infinitely better off.

Women with skills they love to employ, with training they mourn not to use, have every right to exert them; so long, that is, as the family is not essentially harmed. They will be serving the world and providing for the contentment of middle age.

For it is middle age itself which brings many a woman to the edge of an increasingly frequent dilemma. She may have been quite serene until then with house, kitchen, nursery. But her children are now grown and living at a distance. Tasks dwindle. Her interests have, perhaps, never been particularly social. She is discontented with gardening and bridge, and yearns for something sturdier to fill her days. (The busy young will not really believe this. They fancy, to begin with, that they will never grow old—a delusion which only time can overthrow. And they are so beset with household chores that the possibility of too much leisure seems a strange matter for complaint.)

For housewives with time hanging heavy on their hands the best assuagement seems to me to be works of charity. For all our wide-flung networks of community chests and Red Cross drives and social security provisions, the age-old lacks remain. The sick still need care. The poor have to be helped. Orphans want comforting. The schools and hospitals are short-staffed.

But women are human, and not every female creature is by nature a Florence Nightingale or a Saint Fabiola—that bustling Roman matron who established the first free hospital in the West and who was also of so sociable a nature that her friend St. Jerome said wryly of her, "She thinks the lonely Stable at Bethlehem should be merely an annex to the Inn."

Perhaps not good works but a job is the very thing to brace the spirit and engage the mind for able Mrs. Smith down the street who now sells real estate, or for Mrs. Le Blanc who used to run the PTA so efficiently and has now set up a dress shop. Moonlighting can be therapy, not competition; and who would deny healing to the individual psyche?

By and large, though, the world runs better when men and women keep to their own spheres. I do not say women are better off, but society in general is. And that is, after all, the mysterious honor and obligation of women—to keep this planet in orbit. We are the self-immolators, the sacrificers, the givers, not the eaters-up, of life. To say to us arbitrarily, as some psychologists and propagandists do, that it is our *duty* to be busy elsewhere than at home is pretentious nonsense. Few jobs are worth disrupting family life for unless the family profits by it rather than the housewife herself.

You will notice I say "job", not career. I have scarcely mentioned that ambiguous word "career." Career implies, or should imply, peculiar talent, overwhelming and singular accomplishment. The woman with a wood thrush in her throat, the one pursued by a story to tell, a picture to paint, or a scientific theory to demonstrate, stands on different and more dangerous ground than other people. If she is passionate enough about her will to create not a home but a work of art, she will never stop even to consider what is best for the world. The word "housewife" applied to her is usually a misnomer. She is an artist or a scientist who happens, maybe, to have a husband and children. Her problems are always unique and have no place in this discussion.

In between her and the wholly dedicated homebody are the people like me—the part-time writers, illustrators, musicians whom premarital impetus has sent jogging along in two jobs because we don't quite know how to stop. Basically we are housewives who work at other occupations only in our spare hours, as other people embroider or collect snuffboxes. What I would like to tell the young women who see us performing and think that we are having our cake and eating it is that the cake is very hard-won and not so tasty as it looks. We give up a good deal that we enjoy. We miss the easy social intercourse of daily living and are frequently lonely. We work far harder than most women and many men. We are constantly interrupted, intruded on, split half a dozen ways. Sometimes we do as I did and give over our second profession for a number of years for the more vital domestic one, picking it up again, awkwardly and with difficulty, only after the children are grown or off to boarding school or college. We manage because, in effect, we are willing to sacrifice tea parties and matinees and manicures and small feminine pleasures for the dubious rewards of seeing our names on the spine of a book or in the corner of a painting. There are compensations. One of them is the extravagant attachment most of us acquire for our kitchens and hearths, as if they renewed our depleted souls.

"Writers," one of them said once, "make good wives. They are romantic, industrious, and grateful."

The remark has no more authority than any other epigram. But it happens to be true of a number of women I know who write or paint or make music as well as hold a household together.

But then my sort never believed we had a duty to express ourselves as individuals at all cost. We moonlighted because someone wanted us to—an editor or an agent or a husband. I have one painter friend who was spurred on because her children insisted she had talent. I know a novelist who stuck to her typewriter because whenever she wanted anything new and expensive—a fur coat, ballet lessons for her daughters, the best schools for her sons—her husband said cheerfully to her, "All right, honey, you can have it. All you have to do is work a little harder."

It made for a harmonious if busy household, and for a solvent retirement.

So I would have to say to that panel at the club I never visit, only a qualified "yes" to its question. Of *course* women have a right to work if they can do so without stinting the family. They have also an equal right to spend their forces domestically and privately if they so incline. It is foolish of some idealists I know to think the world will change if only women will play a bigger part in it. Women are exactly as silly, brave, farsighted, ignorant, human as men. We have had the vote in America for more than forty years and have made no impression at all on the nation or the universe. We have altered no abuses, improved no political situations. We have not abolished war or poverty or crime or unhappiness. We have simply doubled the voting population. Once that idea is hammered into feminist skulls, perhaps we will be let alone to continue the one career which is truly and uniquely ours.

THE HOUSE

6 ❧ *A Roof of One's Own*

It is perfectly possible to be a housewife without owning a house. Some of the most romantically domestic women I know have lived out their lives in rented apartments where heat came delivered by courtesy of City Steam and gossip got carried around by doormen with the morning mail. Female creatures are born nesters. Give them anything walled and covered over from the weather—a cabin, a tent, a trailer, even a dormitory room in a New England women's college—and most of them will manage to turn it into home. They will decorate the walls, invent a rug or a table, plant something green in a pot, and settle there snug as mice in their burrows.

Still, the desire for a personal roof, however mortgaged, is natural to all mankind. It is more than desire, it is instinct. The human race has always felt safest inside private walls or standing on a bit of owned earth. Only a rare and incorrigibly urban heart never stirs with immemorial longings, has never urged its owner to arise and go now to some local Isle of Innisfree, there to plant nine bean rows, keep a bee, and put up summer screens. So in this affluent day most American families will at some period in their lives go house-hunting. Since that hunt is half instinctive, they are likely to begin that search in the spring, when the sap rises, the flicker builds, and human hopes irresistibly burgeon. No suburban landscape is complete in April or May without its bands of searchers, addresses in their hands, trudging from listing to listing. In this green and flowery county where I live, I watch them come like swallows every season, pilgrims in search of a domestic Grail.

They come in all shapes, sizes, conditions, and degrees of prosperity. Some are veterans of the chase already, either families on their way up in the world who have outgrown modest acquisitions and hope for something more elaborate, or else the middle-aged whose houses have outgrown *them.* Some are strangers, transfers from other cities to this vast suburban area, bewildered by our fashions and our prices. A few are old residents, restless for a change of street. The majority, though, are untried novices, young couples with a child or two or three and very little notion of the hazards of property-owning. They have saved a bit of money, have been elated by a promotion or a bonus. A genuine nest seems within their expanding reach. It is those latter innocents whom I long to warn against searching too optimistically and with too dogmatic a hope.

It is not that they have been, in the main, badly briefed. Most of them have met with lawyers, talked things over with bankers, confided in real estate brokers, even consulted their own relatives. Still, they are innocents, for I know the image each carries in the mind's eye. What they are looking for is a Perfect House.

I can even describe that image. It will be a neat, new, sound, and enduring residence, miraculously mingling the appeal of period architecture with the convenience of contemporary. It will be small enough to take care of without help but commodious enough to shelter a growing family. There will be a garden and a lawn guiltless of crabgrass, but the grounds will require nothing more to keep them immaculate than a weekly mowing. Inside, the kitchen will be modern to the last shelf and counter, the living room admirably sunny and spacious. There will be bedrooms enough for now and for the future, a nice new furnace, a sufficiency of baths, closets, electric outlets. The upkeep will be minute, the neighborhood good. And it must be cheap, a Bargain.

Death and taxes are no more certain than disillusion for them. It will begin on the first morning of the search and continue to the final day when they find themselves in possession of a deed for something as different from that original mental sketch as a film star from her press photographs. For there is no such thing as a perfect house. (What one thinks of as perfection is merely what other people are living in.) On the market they will find all sorts of dwelling places pleasant to inhabit—gracious houses, convenient houses, beautiful houses; houses suitable, impressive, appealing, economical, unusual, or a Good Investment. But perfection is as rare in a building as in a person, a poem, or a marriage. Even if those pilgrims had time and money enough to choose an acre or so of land, hire an architect, engage a contractor, and try to flesh out their private vision, something in that process would go astray. Closets would turn out to be too many or too few, the basement stairs desperately steep, the bathroom tiles objectionable. No doubt King Louis complained of Versailles and Blenheim didn't quite suit the Duke of Marlborough. In every human project there is bound to be a human flaw. After all, the most nearly perfect edifice in the world is the Taj Mahal, and that is not a house but a tomb.

So their choice will be a compromise. The odd thing is, though, that they will settle there in most cases contentedly, sometimes with rapture. For what they will have found out is that they didn't need perfection, only a house which was right for *them.* Buying a house is like getting married. The youthful dream of the Ideal withers and is forgotten. Propinquity, kindness, availability are the things which count. And then of course the important matter is to lose one's heart.

I know because I too have been a pilgrim; indeed, have never ceased to be one. Our family search was more whimsical than I would advise for others, begun on impulse and with rash lightheartedness. For May was nudging us, or at least it was nudging me. The grimy ailanthus tree outside the window of our New York apartment kept reminding me how nice it would be to see two trees or even a whole row of them. My husband, a man who dislikes change, plumped for the status quo.

"Who wants to commute?" he argued. "Time enough to leave town when we have children."

Even when a certain queasiness before breakfast on my part suggested that the offspring in question might soon cease to be an academic problem, he continued to insist that a larger apartment was all we needed. Accident seconded by nostalgia changed his mind. While looking for that extra room in the city, one which would be within our small means, we came across an oddity. It was a tiny private house in Mahattan. It had four floors and exactly four rooms, one to a story. We thought it reasonable, chic, and amusing. We also knew it wouldn't do. Who could isolate an infant on a separate floor or bring a pram up three flights?

Still, my husband tramped down from an inspection of the premises and announced, just as if it had been his idea all along, "Let's go to the suburbs. I want a place where I can walk up and down stairs again."

The next day we took a train to Westchester County, enrolled ourselves under the banner of the first dealer we encountered, and began to learn the hard facts of home-buying life. Of course we knew what we wanted—exactly what I have outlined as the dream of every novice purchaser. But we discovered almost at once that with a bank account practically nonexistent and an income which would stretch no better than wartime elastic, that neat, small, new, sound, and enduring residence was out of the question for us. The operative word is "small." There is and always has been a correlation between size and price. The bigger the house, the less, proportionately, you will have to pay for your purchase. When we were on safari in the late thirties, the Depression lay like a London fog over the whole nation. But even in that era the tidy small house with low taxes and easy maintenance had lost little value. It had kept its owners solvent; they did not need to give it up for lack of income. This village where we finally settled was dotted then with huge, handsome, deserted estates going for a song; for less than a song—a whistle. I remember one in particular, a true mansion with tennis courts and a swimming pool, which sold for four thousand dollars, about the amount of its annual taxes. Who could keep it up? Only the rich, who always get the best buys because they can afford them.

There was nothing, it seemed, for us. So what did we do at the end of our first season of search? Something, considering our natures, astoundingly practical. After being first swept along by a tide of hope, then nearly drowned by waves of disappointment, we decided to tread water. In an amiable and elm-shaded village we found a house for rent. We leased it, giving ourselves a chance to test our needs, our capabilities and deserts. We took it chiefly because the rent amounted monthly to about what it would take now to get a car washed. Looking back on it, we realize it was a terrible house. It had the necessary stairs, three or four flights of them, impressive and battered. It also had twelve rooms, only two baths (one of them dating back, I think, to the invention of plumbing), and a river in the basement when it rained. There were silver knobs on the sagging, genuine-mahogany doors but the kitchen was twice my age and not so well preserved. I'll say for the house, it was well ventilated. You seldom had to open a window, since air blew in unsolicited around every door and casement. Still, we had a fine, gay time there for a year, borrowing furniture from all our friends and relatives to fill it, inviting whole parties of contemporaries out to enjoy the mosquitoed country air, promising ourselves that the sensible little house we yearned for would turn up any day. And one thing we had accomplished without knowing it: we had found our locale. This village where we had lighted by random good luck was where we wanted to stay, with its venerable trees, agreeable neighbors, and stretch of sand beside Long Island Sound for swimming from. (Environment, for a pilgrim, is as important as the choice of house itself.) With our first daughter born and safe in her play-pen, we began again to spend weekends tagging after shepherding realtors.

This time we were better equipped for buying. Our hopes were less high, our savings had grown, we were prepared to purchase with sweet reasonableness. And then happened to us what must happen to all searchers if they are to be content with their lot, not to speak of their house. We fell in love.

On paper the match was not at all suitable. The house was too old, too large, too inconvenient to fit our plans. The well-instructed broker hadn't even bothered to show it to us, since it fit none of our specifications. But one Sunday on an April stroll we passed it, peered over its high privet hedge into a spring garden, and kept coming back almost unwillingly to look at it again, like the reluctant lovers we were. Since it was unoccupied, we even found an unlatched door and feloniously entered, to wander over its three floors and ten rooms, wistfully wishing it were a *little* newer, that the kitchen weren't *quite* so gaunt, that two of the three bathtubs were not standing implacably on turn-of-the-century Chippendale feet. It had so many other features which enchanted us—the nearly half-acre of grounds, the eccentric charm of its old-fashioned rooms, its hale if elderly foundation, which passed my husband's inevitable test for good construction: when he jumped up and down on the floors, neither they nor the walls wavered a hair's breadth. Inquiring about taxes, we found them modest, and we had already learned the asking price was low—for good and sufficient reason. Nobody else except us wanted it. The place had stood empty for more than a year while pilgrims streamed through it, turning away in dismay from four fireplaces, four flights of stairs, and an interior painted throughout a dismal, forbidding green. It nearly dismayed *us*. But we had been delighted by its outward aspect and were encouraged to see through inner gloom to pleasing proportions and fine quality. Out of date or not, oversized or not, the place had charm. And charm in a dwelling is like charm in a woman. It is a mysterious essence compounded of warmth, character, and a welcoming countenance.

"It's a sort of bloom . . . ," says Barrie's Maggie in *What Every Woman Knows*. "If you have it, you don't need to have anything else; and if you don't have it, it doesn't much matter what else you have."

Investment dealers might scream at such flimsy reasoning for making a purchase. Other people might sensibly say charm can't keep rain from penetrating shingles or make up for a nonfunctioning furnace. We agreed and agree, but think also that neither will excellent plumbing and push-button doors make up for trite or graceless architecture.

The right house, no matter what its period, must pluck you by the sleeve and say, "Take me. We were meant for each other."

Which brings me at length to the heart of my argument. The house was meant for *us*, not for our friends or our advisers or our relatives. Indeed, my brother, visiting us here (for of course we bought it; nothing could have stopped us except bankruptcy), grumbled after he had returned to his brisk new ranch house in California, "I can't think what those kids mean, rattling around in a rambling old relic." But we were happy as meadowlarks. We had married our house for love.

Once the honeymoon was over—that is, the delirious first few weeks when we were joyful for mere ownership—there came a natural letdown. Young homeowners must be warned. The six months after moving into a house is likely to be a trial of fortitude. You encounter drawbacks you hadn't dreamed of. You find flaws. Taps don't run, the heating system baffles you, furniture doesn't fit, windows rattle, tiles truculently dislodge themselves. You'd willingly sell back your property to the first honest bidder. But that phase doesn't last, either, for you and your house become friends as well as lovers. Again, it is like marriage. To ensure success, affection and respect must both be present. You must accept your choice for better or for worse, flaws and all, trusting that in the dear one an accumulation of virtues will outweigh the accumulation of faults.

Both virtues and faults we found. The house at once enchanted and exasperated us. The windows were too large and too many, making furniture arrangement a puzzle and adding to bills for storm sash and weather stripping. All that glittered was not copper. There were insufficient shelves for our books, cupboards for our dishes. We were forced to buy a new boiler. But then, we consoled each other, every marriage is costly at the outset. And on the plus side we discovered how accommodating was this aging structure, how impervious to heat and cold. It was solid, generous, full of light, adaptable to change.

Gradually and as we could afford it or had time for do-it-yourself projects, we took advantage of this flexibility. We shelved a library, painted everything bright and blithe, put in necessary kitchen counters, made a dinette out of the dark, butlerless butler's pantry. We tightened things and insulated things and made ourselves so proof against storm that we now heat all three floors for less than three hundred dollars a year—and in spite of the fact I am one of those people who reach for a sweater even on summer evenings and keep the thermostat at a sybaritic 75 degrees day and night in winter. But for all our bits and pieces of change, we let it stay what it was, a stout, unpretentious late-Victorian country dwelling, made of good materials and with workmanlike care.

In other words, we came to terms with our house; like cautious partners in a marriage, we improved but did not try to re-form. For you can enlarge and adorn and coax along the singular object of your choice, but you cannot alter essential nature. Don't buy—and don't marry—unless you are willing to put up with the qualities, good or bad, which attracted you in the first place. This clapboarded shelter of ours will never be smart but it is steadfast. It has housed us happily for twenty-five years. It pleases us still. And its value today is a good deal more than when we acquired it. To finish off the matrimonial figure of speech, you get back what you put into a partnership.

I repeat, our selection would not now or ever be right for all. There are people to whom contemporary design and pristine plaster are necessities. They will sacrifice a dining room for the sake of a built-in kitchen barbecue, prefer 220 wiring to a deep foundation. And since it is they who must live with and inside their own four walls, their choice is proper. At the risk of special pleading, though, I would like to urge the young in search of the few bargains left in the world to consider the case of the dowdy, elderly house. (Of course "elderly" is a relative term. In our area it refers to anything built in the last half-century. Only when it has survived the Revolution do we concede it is old. Yet I know a nest-hunting couple, settling in Arizona, who wrote their parents they were thinking of buying "a very old house, one built nine years ago.")

Not only is something constructed before 1914 inclined to be sold at a modest figure, it is also likely to be low in taxes, since taxes are assessed by age and purchase price. And to someone with an eye for the solid and enduring, this period has satisfactions. What splendid beams carpenters put into buildings then! What deep, dry basements, commodious attics, sunny bedrooms, hospitable porches! (I could write a whole elegy on the passing of the front porch, that comfortable, functional, neighborly appendage, so much more useful in most American climates than a patio or a terrace. Someday, I piously hope, it may return.) They trimmed ceilings and lintels then. They recessed their windows if not their radiators. They made unwarpable doors out of huge slabs of wood. And generously they planned room for children, servants, guests, and in-laws. In such a house the population can explode all it pleases. There are closets. There are pantries. There is privacy. And having stood stalwartly for several generations, without crumbling or settling, it will probably last as long again, losing no value as the years pass.

A surprisingly large group of young pilgrims are discovering the advantage of such houses for themselves now and are deserting the subdivisions and the modish split-levels for an area such as ours. We run to large families here, four seeming a meager endowment, and the new generation of nest-builders are coming across big, undistinguished places for no more than they would pay elsewhere for a two-bedroom, freshly run-up bungalow. These valorous couples are not intimidated by stairs, lavatories less than modern, an absence of air conditioning. They realize they can repair a roof for less than the cost of expanding an attic. They can build their own terraces and improve their own kitchens. Embellishments will come with time.

They appear also to know by ear what we did not learn until we had been in residence more than a dozen years—that no house in which adolescents live is ever too large. Buckingham Palace might well seem crowded while a family is growing up, might burst its seams and strain at its rafters. There will seldom anywhere be beds enough or bathrooms enough or a sufficiency of telephones for the gregarious teens; rarely a place for parents to hide from the sound of records, radios, hair dryers, and high-keyed conversation.

Our newcomers understand this and have chosen space over fashion. Their visions of perfection do not die but are merely put away in the mothballs of the mind. Everybody, no matter how happily sheltered, has a dream house which diverts idle hours and keeps him casually in perpetual search. I have one of my own.

Since I have spent a quarter of a century or more planning it, my dream is quite distinct. I know it is Georgian, new, and made of brick. I am sure it has a view of water, presumably the Atlantic Ocean. The rooms are few but high-ceilinged and spacious, and all of them cluster on one floor. There is a paneled library for those hundreds of books we *will* keep buying, a splendid linen closet such as I have never owned, and place for my husband's enormous piano, now overpowering the living room. When I am feeling opulent, I design a study for myself such as I have always longed for and never attained. There is certainly a laundry unit I don't have to descend cellar stairs to operate. Just contemplating that house has warmed me for years like a hearth fire.

The only trouble with dreams is that they change. I saw mine the other day and did not recognize it at first. New? Georgian? Equipped with a modern laundry and matching baths for its bedrooms? Not at all. I doubt if it even owns a linen closet. The only water view there consists of a glimpse of a duck pond in the middle of a country field. It is two hundred years old, the rooms are tiny, the ceilings immoderately low. Where we could put books or a piano or my typewriter, I can't think. Not at all the house, one would say, for a middle-aged pair to consider living in when their plans involve retirement and an easy existence.

But here we go again, having hopelessly lost our hearts. How do you flout true love?

7 ❧ *A Mind of One's Own*

If buying a house is like getting married, furnishing one is like bringing up the consequent family—a process tricky, demanding, and interminable.

I say interminable with full knowledge of what the word implies. Other and cleverer housewives may quarrel with me here. It may be they have the skill (and the means) to occupy their first four walls with full self-confidence and without tears. Even before they move in they are able to paint all their rooms in colors that do not distress them, select wallpaper which looks just as charming at home as it did in Schumacher's sample book, place their sofas in suitable positions, arrange each bedroom conveniently, hang appropriate curtains from basement to garret, lay down harmonious rugs, and turn the key of the front door onto something with which they can live happily ever after. I belong to a different species. In this beloved but willful house where we have lived so long, the battle has gone on since the day we took possession. Nor has it ever really been won. I get the downstairs done to my pleasure and it's time to start the neglected upstairs. By the time that second floor is finished, everything in the living room needs attention all over again. Nursery turns into study, then into a young girl's bedroom, and back into a study. Guest rooms are metamorphosed into storage cupboards. Books overflow shelves and we have to make a porch into a library. Carpets wear out, draperies fade, paper cracks, we acquire furniture which displaces other furniture. It makes for a full life but scarcely a calm one. And I suspect my case is not unique—that the majority of do-it-yourself decorators will recognize my long if delightful chase after the mirage of perfection.

As for the demands and the trickiness, few, I think, can contradict me. Rearing a family or assembling a house, you come up against equal obstacles. Do it by the book and the result may lack warmth. Do it by ear and you are apt to make mistakes. The requisites for success are the same in both cases—a combination of patience, intuition, effort, and devotion. Money is useful, although it is not quite the primary need. An ability to compromise is essential, since houses, like people, are individuals and make individual demands. And it helps, of course, to have taste.

But natural good taste is rare. A few lucky souls have it from the cradle like long eyelashes or perfect pitch. Most of us simply muddle along with our prejudices or our predilections instead. We proceed by trial and error. We work and we plan and we read the instructions and we study other people's triumphs. Then if our surroundings really matter to us, if we are willing to use our eyes and our wits, we gradually acquire what is even better than taste: minds of our own.

It is only the mindless house which is dull. You know as well as I do the kind I mean—the trite and often expensive rooms full of trite, expensive furniture, reflecting no opinions and bearing no stamp of personality. Such houses are frequently in fashion; too frequently. When the mode calls for colonial they are ruffled and cobbler-benched within an inch of their lives. When the vogue stipulates wall-to-wall carpeting, everything, including stairways, smothers ankle-deep in wool. If tureens on the dining-room table are the recommended ornament, every table blossoms with a tureen. Beds match dressers, chairs come in sets, draperies are chintz or silk according to period. The whole effect of such interiors is as handsome—and as lifeless—as model rooms in department stores. A house which charms and welcomes does not need to conform to any current fashion. But it must wear its owner's signature, just as a poem or a picture ought to speak with a personal voice.

At least the houses I inevitably admire *do* wear that signature. They are not necessarily ones I want to copy or to live in. I enjoy them because they mirror the character of the friends who planned them. Two in particular come to mind. One is contemporary, all bright colors, glass panels, Swedish couches, and Finnish chinaware. The other is a farmhouse, only slightly remodeled, and furnished as much like a Maine cottage as its mistress, homesick for her origins, has been able to make it. In each I breathe invigorating air. For that modern house expresses exactly the virtues of the people who live there—wit, color, originality. The other, with its waxed pine and starched curtains, is a gingham sort of house, its kitchen bigger and busier than its living room, its bluntness and understated hospitality a perfect reproduction of its owner's New England qualities. Mind has been at work in each and so has affection.

In the long run, affection counts most. Your surroundings must make you contented, must suit *you*, not your decorator or your guests or the Rx for style. I doubt that many of my friends covet the results of my haphazard struggles. I go to bed in a room painted cocoa brown, and who else wants a brown bedroom? Who else is so eccentric as to live blithely with a shrimp-colored marble mantel in the parlor or draperies turned inside out because I like the wrong surface of the material better than the right? Or a wildly unfashionable flowered carpet and a perfect hodgepodge of periods—Georgian, Victorian, Biedermeier, Queen Anne, Salvation Army Gothic? What other housewife puts a boudoir wallpaper into a dining room, one composed of doves and roses? Yet I am so fond of that sentimental design that when a few seasons ago it began to show signs of disintegrating, I blackmailed the manufacturer (who had meanwhile dropped the line) into finding a few rolls of it left in his storerooms. This attachment to my own choices, made after weeks of agonizing, leads me into weeks of trouble. Once I have made up my mind, I don't want change. I feel offended when things wear out or need replacing and I have to embark on a search for duplicates. Self-satisfied as it may sound, I love my things. What is more, I loved them even before I owned them.

Early in life I had the good luck—or the misfortune, depending on how you look at it—to set my affection on certain inanimate objects. One was a chair. It had belonged to my grandmother, and it may have belonged to hers. I found it in an attic I prowled as a child, and, probably because it was so different from the stolid mahogany and golden oak which were my everyday environment, it entranced me. A good specimen of early Victoriana, graceful and comfortable (if you don't mind, as I do not, sitting bolt upright), it lacked the hysterical curlicues with which craftsmen of a later period, once wood-turning machines were invented, disfigured their furniture. When I first laid eyes on it, black horsehair intimidatingly covered it, but nothing could disguise its innocent prettiness or the sheen of its hand-rubbed rosewood. The Victorian style has become since then a minor rage and as subject to overexposure as all fads. However, when I fell in love, it seemed unique and I always remembered it. Shortly after my marriage, on a visit to the aunt who had inherited it, I coaxed it back into my possession. My husband and I lugged it all the way to New York as gratefully as more sensible people might elope with treasury bonds. In fact, we pulled it apart leg by leg and arm by arm; and since it had been made with wooden pins instead of nails, dismemberment did it no harm. Put back together again, its oval back and seat upholstered in tufted velvet, it became first an amusing confection and then a focus for our decoration.

The other object of my devotion, and an even more persistent influence, was a set of pictures. Again, I discovered them young. Have you ever read a book called *Cranford?* Probably you have, since its title occurs regularly on high-school reading lists. I, the product of an excessively bad education, had never heard of it until I routed it out of a glass-fronted bookcase when I was recovering from something unoriginal like a midwinter cold. It was only a reprint of Mrs. Gaskell's small classic. But it contained eight full-page color plates by a certain Miss Sybil Tawse. (I am not being formal. That's the ladylike way she signed herself.) The plates were watercolor illustrations of rooms, the rooms in a Cranford Rectory. There were careful delineations of Tudor cabinets, Queen Anne wing chairs, country Chippendale stands, gate-legged tables, cupboards full of blue willowware, embroidered fire screens, pierced brass fenders. I think Miss Tawse meant her pictures to look quaint, old-fashioned in a heterogeneous fashion, as if Cranford people never threw out anything but simply assembled and inherited. To me they were representations of pure delight. I carried the book as well as the yearning for old furnishings with me into my own first home. And I did my best to gather about me pieces as much like Cranford ones as possible.

At first the possibility was slight. Impecunious young couples cannot afford to buy even copies of Queen Anne wing chairs or gallery-topped tables. What we could and did do was to haunt the secondhand stores, attend the auctions, and now and then come across a bibelot which reminded us of the illustrations. In solvent times we occasionally bought a reproduction. But what we found most easily at little cost was Victorian to match my grandmother's chair. Since our first apartment was half a floor in a remodeled brownstone building, Victorian went very well with its peculiar assets—soaring ceilings, white marble mantel, long, narrow windows. We used to spend all our Saturdays searching junk shops for bargains. And in that Depression day, bargains we often got. We also acquired something more useful than possessions: a feeling for quality, some sense of style, and a knowledge of how much to pay for antiques or semiantiques.

We worked out a rough rule of thumb for buying. It was this: never pay more, and preferably less, for something old than you would have to pay for its modern copy. The rule would not work for real collectors. Authentic Sheraton, pedigreed Hepplewhite, bring their weight in rubies. But pedigree is not everything. For a tiny outlay we were able to find a carved rosewood sofa as early and as unornamented as my chair. We picked up for a few dollars a sound Federal sideboard, chests of drawers designed by no famous artisan but well and truly put together, and enough assorted Victoriana to set us up in housekeeping.

Along with our few modest treasures, we also lugged home, quite knowingly, some outright junk. For we quickly formulated a second rule, one we have found useful to this day. We would buy either something so good it would please us forever or something so cheap we could afford later to throw it away. It's not a bad discipline for young householders. It's where the patience comes in. Money may not be your chief lack; inexperience can lead one into as many dead ends as insolvency. It is always well to go slowly at first. You have to be willing, of course, to live with maybe a child's workstand from the Thrift Shop in lieu of a coffee table; you may have to put up with lamps from the ten-cent store. You make do with a draped orange crate for a nightstand and secondhand bedsteads and camp stools in place of dining-room chairs while you wait for the precise and precious objects you have in mind. But if you proceed on this theory, you won't find yourself in trouble five or six years later, saddled with a houseful of mass-produced maple or Department Store Modern which you have grown to detest but which cost you so much you can't bring yourself to jettison it.

You also have to be brave enough to buy on impulse. Most of the things we value have been so acquired. I remember, when we were living in our first two-and-a-half-room apartment, once bidding on a marquetry secretary at an auction. It was a slow day, and my bid of fifty cents over my opponent's offer got me the piece. I brought it home by taxi, and only on the way did I suddenly say to myself with astonishment, "But we already *have* a secretary!"

Fortunately my husband is an easy-tempered man. He agreed that my $37.75 had been well laid out and that two secretaries in one small parlor was exactly what every nicely appointed house ought to have. And that reckless and redundant purchase of mine has for many years been my showpiece, practically the only one which real collectors exclaim over.

In the same way, we believe and have long believed that luxury ought to come before necessity. A delft plate, a Hogarth print, a Staffordshire pug dog, a silver pitcher—if those frivolities are what our hearts pant after at the moment, we buy them in place of bath towels or a dish washer. I owned Waterford glass candlesticks before I had a dinner service. I bought an antique platter when what I really needed was a decent shower curtain. It may not be the way to save up for a solvent old age, but it makes for a cheerful journey along the road.

When we moved from the city to the suburbs we ran into new and different trouble. For one thing, we had to furnish ten rooms instead of two and a half. And they were problem rooms, too tall for their width, too lavishly windowed, cut up into odd shapes and sizes. But I want to give this comfort to the housewife faced with an unconventional house. Problems are a good thing; be grateful for them. As it is the lopsided smile or the irregular profile which gives piquancy to a face, so it is the singular room which is most rewarding to decorate. Necessity is the mother not only of invention but of imagination. I, for one, would not have the faintest idea how to cope with rooms regularly laid out. For the matter of that, I hadn't any idea how to cope with these *ir*regular ones at first. For six months I surveyed my living room, alternating between despair and exhilaration. I used to sit, chin in hand, like Rodin's Thinker, and wonder how in the world I could make it, if not attractive, at least comfortable. For one thing, there was no wall space at all. Two parlors opened out of one another, each nearly as high as it was wide. The pair, between them, owned three doors, seven windows, and two fireplaces. One room had to accommodate my husband's eight-foot-long piano. (The piano had been a great bargain, we thought, as we bid on it. Afterwards we realized no one except music-addicted babes in the wood would have wanted it. It belonged in a concert hall.) Wiser women might have worked out a solution better and sooner than I, but the one my husband and I together finally chose satisfied us.

Lack of wall space we got around by setting one sofa at right angles to the fireplace and another boldly in front of a window. The ceilings we lowered by a trick. We painted them darker than the walls and ran a paper frieze around the top of the walls below them. And we pulled the two rooms together by carpeting the whole area so as to make both rooms seem one. We let the piano dominate the back parlor and put our heaviest chairs near it to moderate its ebony massiveness. Our draperies were also a trick, a fool-the-eye ruse. Since each window stood at a different height and was a different size from the others, we chose the tallest, broadest one as our model. Then we cheatingly hung valances several inches above the top of some of them or as many inches on either side as we needed for congruity. Swags dipped over the spaces between top sills and valances and—presto!—every window looked at first glance like every other. Carpeted and curtained, the double parlors were surprisingly serene.

And while we were about our schemes, we learned a fundamental fact of decoration—which is to spend money freely on carpets but sparingly on drapery material. Handsome curtains need not be expensive. You have only to use inexpensive fabric lavishly. Out of necessity I have used all sorts of cloth at my windows in this demanding house—unbleached muslin, sateen, marked-down nylon satin, mattress ticking. So long as the color was right and the material generously dispensed, they were as effective as twenty-dollar-a-yard damask—at least by lamplight.

On the other hand, never, if you can help it, buy cheap rugs. Hard pressed as we were when we moved in here, we laid out a large portion of our minute savings for the living room carpeting. Today it has scarcely a worn spot in it. In the dining room, however, we compromised on something moderately priced and it rubbed down to the canvas in a few seasons. But whatever you buy, make sure the color is right.

For color is the key to all decorative plans. It is the vital ingredient. Color can elate or depress, soothe or irritate, make a charming house out of a dull one or a humdrum dwelling out of something innately splendid. Of course, I am a crank on the subject and something of a trial to my near and dear. Let me get into a hotel room where the color scheme is vulgar and I go into shock. I have been known to rise at midnight to hang towels over the footboards of red-and-orange mock-leather motel beds so I wouldn't have to face them at dawn. I have also been known to stop workmen busy retiling a bathroom and order them to pull out a whole wall of ceramics which had looked pale blue in the sample but which in large quantities vibrated like the Mediterranean. My husband, interrupted in the middle of a business conference to hear my wild voice on the telephone, agreed with me.

"Spend the extra now," he assured me. "It's cheaper than a nervous breakdown."

For to live with something which rasps your sensibilities like crayon on a blackboard is no bargain. Do without a new car or a vacation. But never let economy bully you into putting up with paint or wallpaper or neon-colored tiles which you abhor. Admit your mistake and start over.

I have made as many mistakes as most amateur decorators, probably more. I just learned early on to annul them, as I annulled the Big One we encountered at the beginning of our life here. We had painted the parlor walls a cheerful canary yellow which went well with the auction odds and ends we had brought from town—the yellow-and-gray-striped sofa, green-velvet *bergères*, white lamps and side chairs. Then we came across a great find. It was Mark Twain's library mantel, the shrimp-colored marble tidbit already mentioned. At the outset it cost us next to nothing, since the city mansion of America's supremest wit was being torn down to make way for a new apartment building. We merely paid a few dollars to the superintendent and he thankfully let us trundle it home. Outset, however, was not outlay. Once we got it in place it was the most expensive purchase we ever made. Against the canary walls it glared at us. Whoever entered the room turned seasick. We had to repaint, re-cover the sofa, alter our entire color plans. Still, it was worth the trouble, for when everything was settled down again, after we had combed the paint out of our eyebrows and laid down our flowered carpet, we were so aesthetically satisfied that we have not wanted to change anything since.

The mantel was planned to stress our Victorian theme, for flighty chairs and marble-topped tables at first dominated this house. They suited the rooms and they were, as I have said, the least expensive *good* pieces we had been able to buy. But little by little, as we had more expandable purses and more knowledge, we unconsciously shifted our emphasis. The house began to change without our knowing it. We still went to auctions, but what we brought back was more likely to be Queen Anne or Georgian than something from 1860. We found a wing chair. We bought willowware. We came across tiny pedestal tables. One summer we got abroad at last and discovered Dublin, the last capital in the world where good English furniture out of the old Ascendancy houses is still being put up for sale. From Ireland, instead of tweed and cashmere, we came home with two chests of drawers, three occasional tables, a pair of Hepplewhite-influenced chairs out of a jury room, Lowestoft cups and saucers, antique Wedgwood, and the Chinese platter which now hangs in our dining room.

We remembered the rule, too. Although nothing had

been made later than 1810 (so that there was no duty), we paid less, even including transportation, than we would have had to lay out for reproductions in American shops. Then we had a triumphant clearing. We got rid of things. We transferred things from downstairs to upstairs. Up to the attic or off to sale went the furniture we had been making do with. And when at length I looked about me, what did I have? A blurred but discernible version of a Cranford Rectory. Without being really aware of it, I had translated a childhood vision into reality.

To be sure, the *bergères* would not have sat in Miss Jenkyns' drawing room; the French mode seldom made its way to country parsonages. There were no gate-legged tables, since I dislike the style. But there was the fire screen, the wing chair, the sofa tables, the pierced fenders. Like the comfortable houses of Cranford, ours reflected no period but only our personal affections.

Now we are preparing to move out of it. In the pre-Revolutionary Connecticut farmhouse where we will presently fetch our lares and penates, there are problems enough to keep us contented for seasons, of a kind I have not previously coped with. Now it is low ceilings instead of high ones I must outwit, old random boards for floors, tiny rooms instead of spreading ones. By the book, the period ought to be steadfast Colonial. But no one can convince me that the best of my Victorian will not look perfectly suitable there, or the French marquetry secretary seem inappropriate. It was the way old houses got furnished when they were lived in for a long time—haphazardly and in a variety of fashions.

Anyhow, my mind is by this time unmistakably my own.

8 ❧ *The Pleasures of Thrift*

All virtues are good, but some virtues seem more virtuous than others. Take generosity, for instance. It smells sweeter than lilies of the valley, never goes out of style, and who has it needs very little else. On the other hand, there are moralities set down in catechisms which latterly have almost no appeal at all. Prudence is such a quality, temperance another. In this passionate and abundant age, they are scarcely considered virtues. Classed with them currently, I suspect, is thrift.

Yet thrift is a genuine virtue and one well worth embracing. It is not romantic and has a private worth, but without it there can be little solid domestic happiness. For thrift is neither selfishness nor cheese-paring, but a large, compassionate attribute, a just regard for God's material gifts. It has nothing in common with meanness and is different even from economy, which, although it may assist thrift, is a habit rather than a moral act. Let me see if I can explain my premise.

Economy saves pennies, trims corners, and has a tidy mind. On the household side, it prefers meat loaf to crown roast not because it is tastier but because it is cheaper. The poor may receive economy's handouts, but they will be relentlessly entered on a tax return. Meanness ruthlessly stints the table, lets others pay the check, and when it gives old coats to refugee committees, cuts off buttons and fur collars. Thrift is something else again. When thrift serves stew to the family to ease a budget, it sees to it that the dish is savory as *filet mignon;* and it delights to share with anyone who comes to the door.

Or let me give a stricter example, one I have seen in operation.

Meanness inherits a set of silverware and keeps it in the bank. Economy uses it only on important occasions, for fear of loss. Thrift sets the table with it every night for pure pleasure, but counts the butter spreaders before they are put away.

Thrift saves for the future because the children must be educated and because one must not be a burden in old age; it has no miserliness. Thrift keeps the house painted and the roof in repair, puts shoe trees in shoes, but bakes a jar of cookies for neighborhood children. It is never stingy and never antlike. Thrift is a preserver rather than a hoarder and rejoices in hospitality.

So it seems a pity that the phrase "thrifty housewife" has almost ceased to be a compliment. Even in this flamboyant era, thrift is as essential as ever to an agreeable and generous life; and wives, as they have always done, must bear the most tedious portion of this human duty.

Practiced in the right spirit, it can become a happier thing, indeed, than simple duty. "For all healthy people economy has its pleasures," says George Eliot in her novel *Daniel Deronda.* In place of "economy" read "thrift" and one has a wholesome epigram. There is satisfaction in seeing one's household prosper, in being both bountiful and provident. By nature I am only partially thrifty, alternating between abrupt economies and impulsive spending. But even I can take pleasure in turning linen in its closet often so that bed sheets will be used in rotation and not left to wear at the creases unused. There is nothing of stinginess but only a proper delight in planning meals so that egg whites, for example, left over from a hollandaise sauce will be utilized before the week is out for a meringue or an angel food cake. And it is better than pleasure, it is almost rapture for a gardener, say, to see her carefully garnered grass clippings turning before her eyes into life-giving compost for vegetables or flowers or a lawn. So long as saving does not become an end in itself, it can be as warm a joy as any other.

But it has to be a personal joy which every housewife must work out for herself. My methods of being thrifty (if I ever am) are different from yours because our goals are different and our capacities various. One way of determining thrift is by describing its opposites—avarice and extravagance.

I am aware of my own avarices. I am greedy about books, for instance. Lavishly I buy them, gladly give them away; but I lend them warily. And when I lend them I want them back. Borrow my umbrellas, my clothes, my money, and I will likely not think of them again. But borrow my books and I will be on your track like a bloodhound until they are returned. I am also niggardly about small things like paper, hairpins, Christmas ribbons (I save every scrap, to be ironed out for another holiday), and matches, which I am inclined to stock up on at restaurants I visit. My husband, the most generous of men in other respects, is a hoarder of hardware. He saves old nails, ancient doorknobs, copper sheeting, odd lengths of pipe. Other people are miserly about string or Plaid stamps or leftover food, which they keep in the ice box until it withers.

I have a friend, an openhanded and wealthy woman, who still cannot bear to pay to have her hair shampooed. She washes it herself before she goes to the hairdresser—an economy she learned as a girl. And I know another charming lady who will give you her time or a listening ear but finds it impossible to give away a flower out of her rioting garden. None of these compulsions has anything to do with thrift. They are acquisitivenesses. What *is* thrifty about my book-lending habits, though, is the fact that I keep a notebook in which I jot down the names of the borrowers, the titles of the books, and the date of the transaction. That, you see, is a provident act. It is a polite record I can turn to after a decent interval.

Extravagances differ, too. In our household we lump, under that head, expensive cars and eating out. We like our own food and find it difficult to enjoy overspending for dishes we could contrive better at home. As for automobiles, we consider them a necessary means of transportation but do not care how shabby is the vehicle so long as it runs. In twenty-six years we have bought only four new cars, two of them still in use. Yet I know families to whom eating in style at restaurants now and then is a valuable treat. To them it is not extravagance but a lift to morale.

And I am quite aware that to some a car is a beautiful, a soul-solacing invention, and a shining new one is worth making sacrifices for. Our postman drives a Thunderbird, replaced every season or so. He is childless, his wife works, he is willing to stay home from the movies and sell insurance in his spare time in order to afford it. He *deserves* his sleek chariot, a machine like Keats's melodist, forever panting and forever young. For him it is not an extravagant gesture but a need of the soul. Everybody, in fact, to be thrifty ought to save toward his favorite luxury. For one family it may mean a son's medical schooling. For another it might be a trip abroad or a new tea rose for the garden. (To the mother of Barrie's Little Minister it meant having an egg every day of her life for breakfast; but that was in another world.) Our desire for pedigreed furniture or excursions to the theater or a well-tempered piano is no worthier an ambition than someone else's for color television or an outboard motor. It is the right private use of money or time toward rewarding ends which *is* thrift.

(Of course, one has to have both first in order to save them. The really poor are incapable of being thrifty because they own nothing to be thrifty with. The old remark that "only the rich regard money highly" is perfectly true. How can you nourish a lack?)

In my own case, I am more apt to disburse time thriftily than money. I have neither the vitality nor the hours to spend in department stores or in supermarkets hunting down household economies. I would enjoy the chase if I dared, for I have a good wide Germanic streak of the *Hausfrau* in me (in spite of my Irish name) and like as much as anybody else to feel the smug glow of acquiring a bargain. But I have a trade to follow, an infirm back to pamper. So I do my marketing, for instance, by telephone. It is not the most economical way, and I do not recommend it to haler housewives. Still, the grocer and I are old friends, and I dare say my bills are not much higher than those of other people. Besides, I follow the seasons in my purchases.

Whatever is seasonably ripe or ready is not only cheaper, it tastes better. When asparagus is plentiful and inexpensive, we eat asparagus several times a week. We delight in strawberries and avocados and oranges and mushrooms chiefly when they flood the stores. Through the mail or on advice of the grocer, I keep track of sales and stock up then on canned goods; but I try not to buy more than we can use in the immediate future. Young housewives, like most husbands, tend to get carried away by anything marked down. I scarcely dare let my own husband out alone on an expedition to a chain store—he comes home burdened with cans of boysenberries (which we dislike) or packages of curry powder (which we use sparingly) or gallon jars of jam (which is apt to linger stalely in the bottle) merely because he saw them at a discount. A bargain, though, is only a bargain if it is usable. Thrift takes account of that.

In fact, when I come to think about it, I effect most of my savings by *not* going to the stores. It is amazing how much one can get along without if there is no temptation to buy. I have seldom regretted the bargain dress I came home without, or the extra pair of gloves on sale which would never have matched anything I own but which were priced so enticingly low. And I have my own ways of taking advantage of reductions. There is always January, when every store in the area reduces the cost of its sheets and tablecloths and towels and housewares. I remember to replace my worn ones then, by telephone or letter.

Naturally, I miss the fun of a good search. I leave that to my husband. He is a born shopper, with far more stamina than I, and nothing pleases him so much as to be asked to scour the marts for a gadget—anything from a door hinge to a dishwasher. I have to remind him ten times a winter that he needs a new overcoat. But mention that I have use for a fish mold, a doormat, or an automatic pencil sharpener, and he is off happily to look, price, compare and come home with the best possible contrivance at the lowest possible cost that can be obtained. If time seems less valuable to you than dollars, be thrifty with the latter and expend the former. Apologetically, I will go on my path—taking taxis instead of buses, doing my Christmas shopping in one exhausting day at one exhaustive store, and ordering my meat over the phone.

Though now I come to think of it, I do not really apologize for the last; the man I patronize delivers anyway. And so long as we have a dollar in our purse, I will go on buying from the same independent butcher I have known and relied on for a quarter of a century. It would be my final economy to purchase meat which has not been selected, cut, and hung by an expert and personal hand. We would rather eat tuna fish and noodles any day than a tough steak; and that is exactly what we do whenever we feel insolvent. A good stew is far more delicious in our opinion than a poor roast or a juiceless capon. And for any other household where food is held in esteem, I give this one strong bit of counsel: save on staples, stock your larder with bargain items in cans or packages, but when you want prime meat, see that it is really prime. If you wish to economize, eat creamed dried beef, which, when bought in bulk instead of in jars and served with a mushroom sauce, is not to be despised. Serve hamburgers. Braise chicken hearts with onion—a gourmet's dish and as inexpensive as cornflakes. Eke out your menus with things concocted of rice. Then, when you feel expansive enough for tenderloin, be lavish as a king and spend for a real feast —something tender, costly, and epicurean.

(Remember, too, that meats and fish, as well as vegetables, have their seasonal cycles. Lamb is best and cheapest in the spring, lobster in the fall. Chicken grows most succulent in summer. And local foods, like a wine of the country, always have the kindest flavor.)

As a matter of fact, the same reasoning applies to nearly everything in life—that quality pays. If it is quality you enjoy, buy sparingly but of the best. I would rather, for instance, have one dress a year and have it fit and become me than own a closetful of clothes in which I took no pleasure. I do not want skimpy curtains at my windows or an ersatz piece of silverware. I would sooner eat on a card table—as in fact we once did for several pinched months when we were first married—than settle for an article of furniture cheap but detestable. I do not mean to imply that everything in our house is either expensive or beautiful—but at least it is as unugly as I can find or afford. It is *my* form of thrift, the patience to wait for what I want. And I have discovered that every time we have made a domestic purchase cheaply and in haste—a shrub for our borders, that important carpet, a bathroom scale—we have repented at leisure. The carpet wore thin before its time. The scale did not measure accurately; the rhododendron turned out to be nonhybrid and undistinguished.

Thrift is a worldly virtue, and it operates by an immutable worldly law: you get what you pay for. To cut corners is not always to cut eventual expenses.

So the thrifty housewife will pay willingly for quality. But once she possesses, she reveres it. Her good durable carpet is preserved against the moth; her well-fitted frocks hang in her closets under plastic covers and have their hooks and eyes and zippers in good repair. (I wish I could say the same of my own.) The herbs in her cupboards are arranged alphabetically, not only for the sake of handiness but because a gap between mace and rosemary will remind her to reorder paprika. She airs sweaters and washes blankets and feeds wax to her furniture. She is clever with leftovers and makes stale bread into crumbs to store in the refrigerator. The refrigerator itself is defrosted in its proper season.

And she is as careful of her time as of her cherished objects. She does not so wear out her days with committees and charitable teas and garden clubs and tracking down bargains that in the evening she is cross to the children and abrupt to her husband. She does not insist on doing her own housework and then complain of being a martyr to the home. If she spends all afternoon icing a birthday cake, she makes sure the effort does not ice her disposition, too. There is nothing chillier than an economical and systematic housekeeper more in love with neatness than with peace.

I have a friend who is incorrigibly absentminded about dusting and sweeping and polishing. She forgets to mend her napkins, lets cobwebs accumulate in corners, and is apt to hem up her slips with safety pins. Once I drank coffee there and set down my cup and saucer beside her fireplace. When I looked in a week later, the dishes were still exactly where I had left them. Nobody could call her a provident housewife, in spite of her excellent cooking; but maybe she has her own vision of thrift, since nothing but kindness and good spirits centers in that house, and her family has never gone hungry or unloved or a guest uncomforted.

But then, I repeat, every woman has to learn to be thrifty in her own idiom. Her economies must be like her luxuries —cut to the shape of the family budget or the family dream; and they must never descend to indignities. Thrift implies dignity, the importance of human worth as well as of inanimate things. It might lie for one person in a thing so small as properly balancing her checkbook or for another in something so large as learning to make all the draperies for her windows. It might consist merely in putting a net over her hair at night to save the curls she paid for, or in being so clever about the food money that she can buy her husband, out of savings, the ivory chess set he has been coveting. I think I demonstrate such thrift as I have in staying doggedly home at my typewriter instead of lunching with my friends. It is not so dramatic or so visible a household symbol as my beloved soup kettle, daily occupied by expendable bones and vegetables; but it is my individual contribution.

The thriftiest of my friends is a woman of limited means. She has lately taken to doing her own laundry in order to mail a monthly check to an impoverished Italian family in Naples whom she has never met. Perhaps in her case thrift has turned into something better; into charity, loveliest virtue in the catalog. Still, the rest of us have to begin somewhere along the road to perfection. Thrift is not charity, yet it can approach it when accomplished with love. And, like laughter or sachets in bureau drawers, it is a pleasant thing to have around the house.

Th[illegible]
ment [illegible]
I c[illegible]
gettin[illegible]
cons[illegible]
an e[illegible]
way to c[illegible]
requires [illegible]
I can [illegible]
emb[illegible]
both [illegible]
It [illegible]
cause [illegible]
eating [illegible]
pain [illegible]
men [illegible]
stairway [illegible]
beam [illegible]
people [illegible]
over [illegible]
the [illegible]
A r[illegible]
hotly d[illegible]

9 ❧ *Party Line*

I love to have given a party.

The sentence above contains neither misprint nor grammatical error. It is a statement of simple truth. In retrospect, I enjoy my own hospitality, believing that to gather together several amusing and articulate friends for dinner constitutes the highest form of civilized entertainment. Once an evening has been irrevocably launched and is well on its way to eternity, the mist vanishes from my eyes, my heart resumes its normal beat, and nightingales sing in the trees. I can tell you approximately the moment when I begin to emerge from a week's trauma and savor the pleasure of being hostess on my own hearth.

It is somewhere around ten-thirty or eleven P.M. The canapés have been passed, the cocktails drunk, the dinner eaten, the ladies coaxed upstairs for gossip and lipstick repair, then coaxed back to the living room to join the gentlemen. I stand for a moment in the hall at the foot of the stairway, listening with suddenly unstopped ears. About me beats the lovely roar of a number of relaxed and uninhibited people all talking at once. As that welcome clamor washes over me, I think as I always do then, that having a party is the nicest occupation in the world.

A few hours earlier—say, at five o'clock—I would have hotly denied such a moment would ever come. Flying about the house in a dressing gown and apron, polishing extra ashtrays, making sure the bathroom towels have not been surreptitiously used, rearranging the centerpiece, discovering that there is not enough ice and signaling a neighbor for reinforcements, propping up candles which insist on leaning drunkenly to one side like the Tower of Pisa, searching for a missing coffee spoon, dazedly tasting the entrée, I am prepared for total debacle. I am convinced that (*a*) the guests will have forgotten the night or will, conversely, all arrive before I am dressed, (*b*) people will hate each other on sight, (*c*) the cleaning woman who substitutes for waitress on such occasions will not appear, (*d*) the mousse will be a failure, (*e*) I must have been out of my mind ever to issue invitations in the first place, and (*f*) after this evening I will retire to a nunnery, leaving the field free for Perle Mesta.

Perhaps you who read this will be hostesses of a different mettle, with steel nerves and hearts of lions, to whom entertaining presents no terrors. If so, what I have to say will seem irrelevant and immaterial. I suspect, however, that the majority of housewives, young or old, are, like me, strung up to the snapping point before the hour when the doorbell rings and the guests surge in. In fact, I have a theory about parties—that tension for a hostess is like stage fright for an actress. It is part of giving a good performance. Only if you are engaged to the hilt in your undertaking, regarding each occasion as important and its outcome valuable, will you be able to compose memorable treats.

It might encourage beginners to know this. I have taken a small census among the friends whom I regard as good hostesses, eminent party-givers. To a woman, they admit that suffering is as necessary to entertaining as vermouth to a Martini—a small but vital ingredient. You have to worry about the guest list, go into a decline when it comes to table arrangements, agonize over the menu, and lie awake at night wondering if the Sewells can really get down from Westport by seven o'clock in the Saturday traffic.

I treasure a remark made to me over the telephone by a pretty and clever lady who lives nearby in our village. Her parties are famous for food and good cheer, and she apparently moves among her guests with the insouciance of a stage star at somebody else's First Night. She even keeps a tame cook. Yet she phoned me one morning, not long after one of her best efforts in the social line, to tell me pathetically that her husband had just been taken to the hospital with acute appendicitis.

"*What* a week it's been," she wailed. "One emergency after another. First the Party and now this!"

Experience helps, but not very much. As a matter of fact, it can be a downright impediment. When I was younger and braver, I can remember asking twenty-four comrades in to eat my turkey Tetrazzini with scarcely a tremor. It was not merely that I had stamina then; I also possessed the hardihood of the ignorant. My standards in entertainment were lower. I had no reputation as a chef to maintain. And I had not yet learned all the perils and pitfalls which can befall a hostess—the delinquent assistants, the guests who slander each other's politics, the extra man ignoring the girl he has been invited to meet, the nervous breakdowns in the kitchen. Still, as one who has come through a number of campaigns, scarred but intact, I do have suggestions to offer about parties in general which may help to sustain someone contemplating her own ordeal.

To begin with, when I say party, you must assume that I mean dinner party. There are other kinds—cocktail parties, teas, luncheons, bridge parties, things horridly called "brunches"; even, I suppose, in more exalted circles, balls and breakfasts. All of them have their uses, even if my own fancy does not embrace them. I go to large teas and mid-week luncheons as infrequently as possible and seldom give them. A few friends in for tea, yes; a crony or two for lunch, possibly; but large, shrill female assemblies intimidate me. Some of my best friends are women. But I consider men as necessary to social functions as vitamins in the diet.

Cocktail parties we have always with us. However, they are usually not parties at all but mass ceremonials designed to clear up at one great stroke a wealth of obligations, rather than to enjoy. Noisy, crowded, and frenetic, they spoil your appetite for dinner, fatigue your larynx, deprive you of the delights of conversation, and hide you from your hostess. What is worse, the supply of chairs is almost never adequate; and as you will see later, I consider the opportunity to sit down the one indispensable requisite for any gala.

Certain cautiously designed cocktail parties in our village I *do* find rewarding in spite of my bias. Friends here have a pleasant custom of getting together early on Sunday afternoons. Ours is an old-fashioned town where nearly everyone goes to church. After the late service at St. John's Episcopal, the last mass at St. Augustine's, the final sermon at what is called the Community Church (and which unites practically all the other denominations), we meet for drinks and canapés about one-thirty, for an hour or two. We greet our neighbors, we gossip, we munch; we then go home to our gardening or our dinners or the Sunday papers, all at a restful time of day. So we eliminate the late-staying coteries and the general dishevelment which makes other such affairs a feat of endurance for all concerned.

And there is one large afternoon party given every year by a witty couple we know which is always a cherished event. They plan it for New Year's Day. Their house is large, so they ask at least a hundred people to drop in at any time from four to seven. They serve hors d'oeuvres, little cakes, and sweetmeats. The only drink is coffee. And there at the end of the week's exhausting revelries and indulgences, we meet to visit and say a "Happy New Year" to charming company. I like the coffee; I like the festive air; and I like the fact that I've always been able to find a seat.

Still, I insist that dinner, and dinner only, is entertainment at its best. The size of the party depends on one's own tastes and resources. If you have a commodious house, plenty of chairs, tables sufficient to seat every guest, and either an adequate kitchen staff or unquenchable vitality, you might ask as many as twenty or thirty people and find the evening exhilarating. My preference is ten. That is a large enough number to seem important and not large enough to be unwieldy. Four I do not consider a party but a family visit. Six cries for formal service. Eight is impossible to arrange correctly at table—work out the mathematics of trying to put a man at the head and a woman at the foot and you will see I am right. Twelve or fourteen overflows the average dining room and demands card tables set up shakily somewhere else, so that the seating protocol becomes a feat worthy of State Department training. Ten is perfect, at once intimate and animated. Everyone will have a chance to talk to everyone else, most houses or apartments will accommodate that number without crowding, and it is possible for you, in a pinch, to both cook and get the dinner to the table with some aplomb.

I must confess that personal prejudice works on me here, too; for my dinner table seats exactly ten with comfort. And let me reiterate with the persistence of a Cato crying out, "Carthage must be destroyed!" that I consider *sitting down* imperative. I don't mean sprawling in an armchair in the living room, either, with a plate balanced precariously on your lap. The young housewife with small quarters may have to serve in such fashion; and when her guests are also young and reckless, the evening will be bearable. But once you have a dining room, the thing to do is to use it. By all means, employ the buffet if you have one. Who, in these servantless days, can depend on a maid to pass from the left and take away from the right and fetch in finger bowls and doilies? The buffet of food is convenient, attractive, and acceptable. But when you utilize it, go right ahead and set up the table too, with glasses and napkins and butter plates and enough forks and salt and pepper.

While you're at it, have place cards. Place cards are not pretentious; they are sensible. It is a rare woman who owns the presence of mind to keep a seating plan in her head and be able to wave her guests into the places arranged for them, at the same time presiding at the sideboard, spooning out the salad, or urging reluctant eaters to try a bit more of the veal *bonne femme*. My talents do not include such tact. I just write out the names beforehand in a sane moment, and expect my friends to be able to read. Thus husbands are segregated from wives and there is no chance for two or three men to huddle together unsociably at one end of the table.

Careful seating is really a matter for concern and one on which I spend as much time and thought as I do on the sauce. It is simple enough to see that the guest of honor perches on my right. It is not so easy to make sure each person will have next to him a charmer certain to please. Still, I do my best to match partners like a pair of gloves, taking into account common interests and mutual enthusiasms. I like also to place the largest and brawniest guest where he will have room for leg and elbow—assure myself he will not be penned between two other active, gesticulating diners. Physical comfort is a part of pleasure. Do not overlook it. If you light candles, arrange them so they will not flicker disastrously in front of blinking eyes, or shut out a view of faces. Make the centerpiece low enough so that the gregarious can talk across table if they like. See that the serving plates are warm, the supplies of everything ample, and that there are cigarettes and matches and ashtrays available for smokers.

I leave the menu to your own resources and imagination. I take it for granted that anyone who has entertained more than twice or gone out to dinner at all will know the elementary facts of party food. She will not attempt something, however enticing it sounds in a recipe book, which she has not first sampled in private. She will forgo the clichés of baked ham and scalloped potatoes, once the standard diet for provincial buffets. And she will make sure the food is varied in texture, color, shape. I once attended a dinner where the hostess had—inadvertently, I trust—

planned everything bland and pallid as a melting snowball. All was white—the vichyssoise, the chicken, the rice, the creamed vegetable, the rolls, the cakes and ices. I even recall the salad as somehow managing to be white, too, although that must have been hallucination. The meal fatigued eye, palate, and, finally, conversation. So when you serve, say, chicken Marengo, leave tomato out of other dishes; see that some lively green vegetable invigorates the color scheme. The same rule holds true with the other qualities I mention. Molded foods are attractive, but don't have a series of them. Vary the textures, so that nuts and mushrooms, for instance, do not occur more than once. Monotony can be as deadly in cuisine as in speech.

The beginner ought also to be warned that an entrée which must be carved at table is often a nuisance, slowing up the procession at the buffet or the passing of plates. Meat which comes in individual portions or which can be sliced ahead of time in the kitchen is best. Hostesses must remember, too, that the salad bowl should be big enough to serve from without spilling, that rice or a noodle ring is easier to keep hot than potatoes, that garlic is a sterling herb but must be used with discretion. Dessert is often a problem, since it takes so much time to assemble if it is to be dashing. When I am pressed for time or tired of my own concoctions, I cheat a little. From a pastry store in our community, I order their specialty—French pastries and fruit tarts in several varieties. These I pass on a large round platter, letting each guest choose his favorite tidbit. I may lose a bit of acclaim, but I breathe easier when I have them safely on hand.

And do pour wine if your pocketbook or your convictions permit. A glass of even a domestic vintage adds something festive to a dinner, lifts it into the party realm.

But more vital than food, more essential than chairs, is the guest list. There may be hostesses who think that merely inviting ten or a dozen people to whom she is indebted and giving them food and drink constitutes a party. I believe otherwise. The only way to assure success is either to ask close friends, bound to find each other amusing, or to study the personalities and dispositions of the invitees and plan around them. Choose your guests as you choose your season's wardrobe, with regard to the style and harmony of the whole. At some point their interests ought to touch, as hands touch when one forms part of a living chain. Those interests need not be vocations. By all means, mingle people engaged in various occupations, in anything from chicken farming to photography, so long as on some subject they speak a common language. The subject might be books or hi-fi or small boats or music boxes or merely the schools their children attend. (I have been at parties which went like wildfire simply because everybody there had bought their houses from the same real estate dealer.) In some province of thought, they must be devoutly and mutually partisan, if it is no more than a passion for early Charlie Chaplin movies.

I was once invited to meet a famous actor. Since the group was to be very small, and since my grasp of theater gossip is about equal to my knowledge of differential calculus, I expected the man would be as wearied by me as I would be awed by him. Yet before we had been together fifteen minutes, we discovered that we had both been operated on by the same doctor in the same hospital.

We fell figuratively on each other's necks with delighted cries of recognition, like two Old Harrovians meeting in a jungle outpost. The evening was too short for our reminiscences. You can't always arrange for such a happy set of circumstances as that, but you can *try* to match the Joneses, who have a rock garden, with the Smiths, who cultivate roses; or to pair off the Johnsons, addicts of jazz, with the Carrs, who own a lot of Bix Beiderbecke's vintage records. If most of your friends are bookish, don't attempt to wean them away from a free-swinging discussion of their preferences in fiction into playing paper games or bridge. Save the bridge or the paper games or the dancing for groups who enjoy those sports more ardently. On the other hand, if you are inviting those who think Faulkner is the name of a sports car, avoid asking in book critics or professors of literature to meet them. Neither set will enjoy the encounter.

I have mentioned ten as being the proper size for a dinner party on account of its malleability. It is also best because ten people of similar enthusiasms are easier to find than twenty. The mixing-and-matching becomes harder as the group multiplies. Yes, I know. If you are a sociable type, you must then go to the trouble of having another party for *another* ten friends. But didn't I warn you at the beginning that you can't entertain without trouble? A successful party is a creative act, and creation is always painful.

Be ruthless, too. Shun the genuine, fourteen-karat bore, no matter how worthy or good-hearted; no matter how heavy may be your obligation to him. At an otherwise sprightly gathering, one invincible, garrulous, grinding bore —the kind who sets your head swimming and your inlays aching—can drag down a whole dinner party as a drowning man can pull his rescuer underwater with his flounderings. We all know, or profess to know, bores who are kindly, Christian men and women, deserving of our respect. I happen to think this belief contains a fallacy. What makes people bores is their insensitivity, their lack of warmth and humor, their inordinate egos. Nevertheless, society is rife with them, and we all number them among our acquaintances. I repeat that you must quarrantine them from your parties. Entertain them with other bores, if you wish to do them honor. Invite them to Christmas dinner. Take them to the theater. Deduct them from your income tax as a charity. Just don't inflict them on the friends whose happiness and health are for an evening in your hands.

In fact, I have come at last to the core of the party line. A dinner should be a time for happiness, a chance for people of like tastes and casts of mind to enjoy each other's company. All should be pleasure—the food and wine and flowers and chairs and candles and, particularly, the conversation. Don't be afraid of where that conversation may range. If you have chosen your company carefully enough, it may range anywhere and still be agreeable. Encourage argument. Let discussion thrive.

Someone once asked my husband if he thought politics was a fit subject to bring up in public.

"Politics? Of course," he said firmly. "There are only three topics people never get tired of discussing. The other two are sex and religion."

His statement was as exaggerated as it was exuberant. But he was partly right. Lively topics give rise to lively talk. The freer, the less trite the conversation, the more happily it flows—so long, that is, as one remembers to class bigots along with other bores and exclude them from social occasions.

And when the talk is good, when there is wit, laughter, banter, friendliness, the hostess gets her eleven o'clock reward. She has planned carefully and taken pains. She has studied her guests and their inclinations. She has served as distinguished a meal as she knows how. Now the responsibility is off her shoulders and she need only empty ashtrays and replenish glasses. She wanders into the hall, perhaps, to tuck a wisp of hair back into place before the mirror. And she hears that heart-lifting roar of talk rolling toward her like a benediction.

It has all been worth it. Her party is a success. If she is a born optimist like me, she automatically begins to plan another.

10 ❧ *Help!*

Our brave new world has not managed to solve all human problems. We are still plagued by crabgrass, unemployment, juvenile delinquency, and the common cold. The servant problem, however, so harassing to bygone generations of housewives, has nearly vanished. So, of course, have servants.

When I was a child, even when I was newly married, it was a rare middle-class household where either an aproned maid or at least a hired girl, talkative and industrious from some outlying farm, did not wash the evening dishes, mind the baby, and give a hand with the summer canning. There were more maids than telephones. Nowadays most of us make do with a set of unlikely substitutes —teen-age neighbors sitting with the children for so much an hour and the use of the refrigerator; occasional part-time cooks driving to work in their station wagons; handymen or "contract gardeners" who mow the lawn or pull up the lobelia borders, along with the weeds, for a king's ransom. The full-time domestic is infrequent enough to be remarkable.

Adaptable as always, housewives get along very well without that extra pair of hands. They have learned to be their own chefs, to flourish a broom or its electric equivalent, put the dinner dishes into a machine, and carry the babies with them when they venture abroad by day. I have friends of my own age who declare themselves happily emancipated by the new era. When they were young and poor they kept help even if they had to go without a new winter coat. It was a part of middle-class living, just as owning a hi-fi set is today. But, "I like it *this* way," they now insist. "I enjoy the privacy and I keep my weight down."

Still, even the most independent woman will occasionally need paid assistance in order to cope with illness, an extended trip, an invasion of guests, or the mere onset of affluence. At some time in her career, she may have to rely on someone beside herself or a member of the family to take charge of the vacuum sweeper or the stove. And she might as well learn early that getting along with that help is a delicate and demanding art. I know. For I am one of the rapidly decreasing little group of diehards who employ a maid when they can, through necessity or choice.

In my case, both apply. It is not just that personally scouring the sink interferes with writing. There are plenty of energetic women who combine the pair of trades without skimping either. But I have two handicaps—one physical, one mental.

The physical is a redundance of backbone. Several years ago a couple of enthusiastic surgeons chipped away part of it and gave me a durable six inches of steel in my spine. It is an operation, one of them told me recently with peals of hearty professional laughter, which "we don't perform any longer." But receiving is easier than giving back in such affairs, and I still go about my ways like an ambulatory lightning rod, while the orthopedists, nothing daunted by experiment, return, as it were, to the old drawing board. I'm fine, you understand; just fine. Only, if I bend over too far or too spontaneously, I can't get up again. So making beds or picking up anything much heavier than a feather duster is dangerous business.

The mental handicap is more enslaving. It consists of an incurable singleness of mind. If I am doing the housework myself, I turn into Old Dutch, complete almost to sabots and pail. Any spot on the wall starts me washing first the spot, then the area next to it, finally the entire surface. I dust from floor to ceiling, not forgetting the slats of the bed. I look at a stain on the carpet and am down on hands and knees cleaning wall to wall. Long ago my family persuaded me that the prudent thing to do was to hire someone else to sweep and scrub so that rust would not take over my typewriter. I try to be myopic about the result, and everyone is happier now that I take off part of the day for what my daughters indulgently refer to as "Mommy's scribbling."

Besides, I like having another woman around the place. I do not really understand my friends when they complain of that invasion of privacy, that dreadful sense of never being alone. If Providence had provided for me on my own terms, I would live in an enormous and populous house, entirely surrounded by children, grandchildren, assorted relatives, and large, cheerful servants bringing in tea trays and giving gratuitous advice. Life can become too private, too enclosed for the soul's good. There may have been injustices and discomfort in earlier days, but a sense of life was seldom lacking. If we still lived so, all generations and estates together, the young might be less self-centered, parents more confident, and Medicare and our current concern for what we horridly call "senior citizens" unnecessary. Now that I have no children at home, I yearn not only for someone to change the sheets and turn out the larder shelves, but for another voice, a different personality from my own to act as counterirritant for the day's vexations. So I hold onto domestic help when I can.

In thirty years I have learned certain techniques of that art, applying equally well to cleaning women, nurses, cooks, or the longed-for all-purpose "housekeeper." (If you are grand enough ever to want a butler or a parlormaid, then you are beyond my orbit, and I have nothing worthwhile to tell you.)

The primary necessity, although you may be reluctant to believe it, is not merely a generous wage. That you pay for what you get is a rule of life. There are no slaveys any more. Maids know their own scarcity value and set their own local scale of payment. Still, offering a bonus or a double salary will not buy a willing heart or an unresentful mind, and you are likely to buy the ire of your neighbors along with it. Once when I was recovering from some illness, I was interviewed by a massive, self-important young woman who asked so startling a weekly sum for her services that I hired her in awe, thinking she must be the paragon for which I had been searching. She could neither cook nor clean, and I thankfully saw her depart after two months. All she had in the way of qualifications was enormous gall.

On the other hand, my husband has for twenty-four summers (with time out for the war) leaned for help on the good right arm of a man so handy that the term takes on new and eloquent meaning. Our Leon can paint, clip a hedge, repair a roof, transplant a tree, or wax a floor with equal efficiency and goodwill. He does factory work in the city during the week and comes to us in the suburbs, as if for a holiday, on alternate Saturdays. A month or two ago my husband was shocked to discover that every other outside man in the vicinity was getting more money than Leon. He had to press the extra two dollars a day on the quixotic fellow over his genuine protests. Evidently what we provided—fresh air, cigarettes, conversation, and a hot midday meal—meant more to him than income.

That midday meal, by the way, is vital if you employ a man instead of a woman for any task around the house. Don't try to fob him off with a sandwich. Give him meat, potatoes, vegetable, and dessert and he is apt to cleave to you though all about you the neighbors were crying for his services. It is not appetite alone. It has something to do with masculine pride and perquisites.

Such minor matters, likely to be disregarded by the inexperienced, often count more than large ones. Any manual will tell you basic rules of employment. One takes it for granted that a "sleep-in" maid will be given her own room, bath, and television; that she will rest in the afternoons and have two free days a week; and that you will provide her with uniforms if she is sensible enough to want to wear them. A friend of mine has had with her a Swiss girl who for six years has stoutly resisted uniforms. She will do anything else—weed the garden, cook for a wedding, drive the children to school, turn the whole house out twice a year for a good old-fashioned cleaning. But uniforms are bound up in her stubborn Swiss mind with menial service, and that she refuses. That particular problem has never come up for me. Anybody who has ever worked here has been pleased to accept the dresses and aprons I buy. They know they are not a badge of slavery; only good economy.

Outside such essentials, however, implemented perhaps by presents on Christmas, birthdays, and when one returns from a journey, there is no need to inflate the average respectable rate of pay. Forget about buying the Ideal Servant. That nebulous figure will come by chance, if at all.

We had an Ideal Servant once. Her name was Cora, and for the most placid five years of my married life, she formed the keel of our household ship. Cora lived with us in the dreadful, splendid days of the Depression, when maids were cheap and plentiful. So I did not know until afterward just how bright a jewel she was. Cora followed Jessie, who worked part-time for us in New York and whom we coaxed into accompanying us to the country when we moved. With her Jessie brought her nine-year-old son. I was full of plans for his welfare, dreamed bountifully of how he would grow and thrive with us. A month of trees, green grass, and air unenlivened by carbon monoxide so depressed the boy that Jessie had to take him back to the streets of Harlem, away from the frightening bees, the birds who woke him up in the morning, and the hideous, alien flowers. Then Cora came.

She was tall, talented, and tireless. I do not know wha

we gave her that she deserved, beyond a small salary and our complete affection. What she gave us was a quick mind, unutterable tact, skill with food, and ungrudging ervice. She left us during the war to do patriotic factory work, got ill, and died. Our skies darkened. Somehow we had never envisioned life without Cora. What it turned out to be, in fact, was life without any help at all. God knows I tried to replace her. There was Mary, who drank up our New Year's Day brandy and dropped the dinner on the floor. There was Esther, who slapped the children. There was Rose Marie, who in two weeks ran up a telephone bill of $84.68 talking to Columbus, Ohio. I also vaguely remember Henrietta, who had been a short-order cook in a diner and who could French fry potatoes or make bacon-and-tomato sandwiches cut into quarters (an olive on a toothpick spearing each section) but not much of anything else. At last I took the sensible course, which today is the course of almost every young housewife. My back was then still flexible, so I bent it toward the ironing and the cleaning and the scrubbing. I learned how to cook, acquiring during the process a lifelong addiction to the habit. But unlike my contemporaries, I continued to miss that other Presence. Once the war ended, I took up the search again and have, as I said, discovered the rudiments of keeping help, if not happy, at least in residence.

I learned the blissfulness of ignorance, for one thing. Before the war, I had been content with anyone who was kind enough to work for me. Now that I had lost my domestic innocence, I noticed cobwebs behind radiators and dust on the tops of pictures. I was discontented with cooks who believed fried chicken and frozen peas the height of culinary delight. But grumbling gets you nowhere, and I taught myself to turn a blind eye on less than perfection. After all, it might be *my* house, but it was somebody else who was keeping it tidy, in her own fashion; and the better part of valor was to swallow my complaints. I correct only by example now, and there hasn't been a cross word between a maid and me in years. If a newcomer, however, is thoroughly impossible, I gently disengage her after six weeks. Six weeks is not enough time to send you to the asylum, and it is sufficient for a trial.

I learned other things, too, not in the manuals. All the books tell you to be explicit in your demands, and I agree. It is not enough to show the incoming Dora or Evelyn or Willy Mae over your establishment, to point out the eccentricities of the gas stove and tell her how to work the electric coffee pot. You have to spell out the time you expect dinner, the way you fold the corners of the blankets, your particular manner of arranging silver on the table. In my case, I bluntly explain also that I am to be allowed into the kitchen to cook when I like. It saves me from future sulks when I come downstairs to make the dessert or assemble the evening's salad.

But the books do *not* tell you something I have discovered—that if you are wise and your candidate is literate, you will draw up a typewritten list of tasks to be accomplished each day; and you will cheat a little. You'll make it heavier than you really mean. It is always easier to withdraw a responsibility than to add to it. Domestic help, like most humanity, have literal minds. If they are told they must clean the living room on Friday, they will resent your asking them, later, to do it on Monday morning, too. If you assure a maid that when you have more than six people at dinner she need not serve, and then invite a seventh guest and expect her to pass the plates, it goes against her grain. Let the job become easier than it looked at first, and she will think her weekly pay not too hard-earned.

And let that weekly pay come personally from you. Never leave it on the kitchen table for her to pick up as she hurries away on Thursdays. Persuade your husband not to dole it out. The hand which pays her is the one she respects; it should be yours. And when you pay, pay promptly. In the bad old days when servants slept four to a bed and twelve-year-old girls toiled up back stairways with jugs of hot water for the gentry's bath, there may have been faithful footmen who worked for love—who waited for their wages from year to year or delighted to lend the young master money from their savings. I suspect they lived chiefly in fiction. The self-respecting domestics of today have bank accounts and mortgages and installments on the television set to meet. See that payday is as inevitable in the home as in your husband's office.

I learned those things. And I learned not to put my faith in references. I once engaged a Cuban girl named Lilith, who came to us with such glowing testimonials from the American Consulate in Havana that I feared we could never live up to her. Lilith arrived, speaking little English, and with a suitcase so heavy my husband staggered carrying it up to her room. Six hysterical weeks later, when she left us—propelled, as it were, from behind—we found out the reason for its weight. Stacked in her closet were twenty-eight empty rum bottles. Recalling our brief affair with Lilith, and the herald of her approach, I sometimes feel our diplomats in Latin America may deserve some of the names called them by Fidel Castro.

Conversely, I once hired a girl whose former employer told me over the telephone that she was "the second worst maid I ever had." The young woman in question was named Eileen, and she had been in this country only a few months from the wild, wet coast of Galway. It was my husband, beguiled by her soft Irish voice, who persuaded me to try her anyhow. For a week or two it was touch and go whether or not I would be driven out of my few wits by her ineptitude. That she could not cook, I knew beforehand. That she understood almost nothing about a toaster, an American stove, or an electric sweeper, I had not been fully warned. In that impatient house where she had worked after debarking from the Shannon plane, they had not bothered to train her for anything except corralling small children. She was, into the bargain, an odd-looking creature; overweight, her hair an uncontrolled curly mane, two front teeth indubitably missing.

But by good luck I persevered. And suddenly as lightning comes in August, she caught hold of the American idea. What she had needed was encouragement, a hospitable household. She was only nineteen, shy, her genuine talents hidden under gaucherie, just as her very good looks had been disfigured by bad dentistry and a starchy diet. She had not wanted to be a nursemaid but a cook. It was her métier: I taught her what I knew about cuisine, and she was miraculously quick. I showed her how to cut her hair, and she, by observation, discovered how to dress. Her weight went down. My dentist repaired her teeth.

At the end of three years she could do everything about the house better than I, including the cooking. She had also turned into an object so decorative that my dinner guests used to think I had hired her for the night from Central Casting. If she had kept her room in a state less chaotic than my daughters did theirs, and had not now and then forgotten to clean the kitchen corners, she might have been another Cora, with an Irish accent. What happened eventually has been forever expressed by the immortal Saki: she "was a good cook, as cooks go; and as cooks go she went."

She went back to Galway on a visit to her family, bearing with her a wardrobe of excellent American clothes and our loving wishes—and with a promise to return in four months. There she met the son of the most affluent farmer in the district, who, as well he might, and with a precipitancy rare among the Gaels, fell in love and married her out of hand. We mourn her still.

But I continue to be wary of references as I am of agencies. Agencies are perfectly suitable to apartment dwellers in cities. In our suburban village, it is the grapevine which furnishes us best with help destined to be friends and companions. A former cleaning woman who stops by frequently for a cup of tea with me has kept me going for years. I hope and believe I am on her list of Favored Employers. At any rate, I know she gives me good references when I am being interviewed. The nicest thing about the grapevine is that those who come by that route are apt to have cronies in the neighborhood—a very important item. There is nothing sadder than a sociable-minded maid with nobody nearby to gossip with after lunch. Making sure she has company is as vital as remembering that she is exactly as mortal as you. She, too, has headaches and depressions and family troubles. The mail does or does not come. The nights are sometimes sleepless. Keep a cautious tongue in your head on her bad days, and mind your manners with domestic help even more carefully than with your family.

And if you are so fortunate as to find a maid you love with your whole heart, you might try binding her to you by having a child or two born during her tenure. Not high wages or Christmas gifts of blue-chip stock or every weekend off will prove so much a lure as children to whom she has grown attached. The only women I know in our village with old family retainers are all mothers of large families. One friend of mine with six boys, I accuse of being philoprogenitive out of desperation. She knows that if she stopped having babies, her famous and wildly competent Evangeline would depart for greener pastures. Evangeline can do everything—order the children's underwear, cook for sixteen guests, repair fuses, call the doctor in emergencies. But her sense of her own importance to that household is less strong than her affection for those six rampaging little boys. Last year my friend and her husband went abroad for the summer. The two oldest boys were scheduled for camp and the next two—a pair of twins—were about to be entered for its junior division. That would have left Evangeline with only a big house to look after and two preschool children to mother.

"But, Mrs. Holden," protested Evangeline, "You *can't* send the twins away. I'd be too lonesome."

If you are unable to supply children, you can at least produce the next best thing, which is praise. Praise is like love: it makes the world move smoothly. Help whom you cannot praise had better not be hired at all or not kept beyond the initial six weeks. If she cannot bake a cake, tell her you enjoy her hamburgers. If she forgets to mop behind the stove, praise her for keeping the sink so sparkling. She is certain to have good points or you wouldn't want her around at all. If you are tactful and industrious yourself, and she is not stupid, she may gradually come around to your way of keeping a house.

At present we are ruled over by Agnes, who came as a "temporary" to fill out Eileen's four months away, and stayed on. Agnes is clean, willing, and eccentric. (I do not fear she will read this, for she scorns all printed words unless they are in her Bible or the World Almanac.) She talks out loud to herself in the kitchen (she tells me that she often wakes herself up at night with single-voiced conversation), dislikes to answer the telephone, and is not, or rather was not, much of a hand with any dish more complicated than bread pudding. She instructed me when she came that she wasn't "a pastry." But by cooking stoutly at her side, by exclaiming enthusiastically when a dish turned out well, by coaxing her into following recipes, we have persuaded her to be quite an adequate chef. The only drawback is that she turns out to be insatiable for praise. She expects it for everything she does, if it is only polishing the silver teapot.

"See, ma'am," she'll say as I grope my way through a

fog of sleep to the breakfast table. "I washed the counters."

Or, "Look how nice I just swept the hall."

Because she has virtues to offset this compulsion, we go along with her.

"Agnes," we tell her fifty times a day, "the bathroom *is* shining." Or, "Agnes, yes, the bacon at breakfast was delicious."

Last Friday we had guests for dinner, and with my tactful assistance, Agnes turned out a splendid meal. So on Saturday morning, my husband—a man with a compliment always ready on his tongue—prepared to build up her ego with a postmortem on the menu of the evening before.

"Agnes," he told her solemnly, "you really outdid yourself. And how the guests enjoyed it!"

Warming to his subject, he began to go over every item with gusto.

"The soup was perfect; not too thick, not too thin. It couldn't have been better. And that baked striped bass! Wonderful. You made the stuffing, didn't you? Well, everybody loved it. Then the asparagus—you cooked it just the way we like it, with the heads whole and the stalks tender. As for your biscuits! Did you notice how we kept having to send back for more? And, Agnes, that cherry pie was a masterpiece. Juicy, sweet, flavored exactly right."

Listening, I silently applauded his stamina as he went on to mention even the coffee and the commercial mints. Agnes listened too, head on one side, ears open and avid. I only hoped he was not heaping on the flattery with too heavy a hand even for her uncomplicated nature. Evidently, though, she hadn't the faintest suspicion there might be teasing mingled with his praise. He ran down, finally, for lack of adjectives. She waited a moment. When she spoke it was with a child's disappointment.

"Yes, sir," she said. "And the mashed potatoes?"

Hail, Agnes! You may not be ideal, but you are here, and I suspect you plan to stay. Anyhow, who expects perfection in this world?

11 ❧ *The Welcomed Guest*

Whatever happened to the guest room?

A query like that scarcely qualifies for inclusion among the Ten Critical Questions of the Decade, but it does nag at the mind. When I was a child, no house which considered itself a house was ever without what was called a "guest room" in worldly circles and in humbler ones the "spare bedroom." There it invariably stood at the head of the upstairs corridor as you turned left, a severe and chilly chamber where wallpaper seldom altered and winter radiators were turned off between occupancies.

A blue-satin comforter, slightly faded, lay folded carefully at the foot of the bed, and blankets lived in bottom drawers aromatic with mothballs. Clamped to the headboard was a fringed reading lamp, and the dresser held a pin tray, a silver bud vase, a powder dish, and an immaculate comb and brush. I do not remember ashtrays. The "little woman" who came in to sew (although the actual one I recall was vast and plump-armed) sometimes moved her sewing machine there for a week of dressmaking; and when young patients were recovering from chicken pox or measles they were permitted to take their fairy tales and coloring books and do their convalescent squirming in that state apartment. The rest of the time it was reserved for visitors.

Nowadays, though, except in the most expansive households, the guest room as an institution seems to have vanished. Have our houses grown smaller, our families larger since the antique days I almost remember? Do guests come to stay less frequently? Or have we turned more self-indulgent and inhospitable than our ancestors? To all three propositions, I think, the answer must be a modified yes. While the population explodes, houses dwindle in size. We who can drive a hundred miles for dinner and back home again do not require a lodging for the night. And there's no doubt about it, we *are* all more jealous of privacy, less willing to be incommoded than were our grandparents. Read a Victorian novel and gasp at the amount and the duration of the visiting which went on before automobiles. Or if you would count your blessings, dip into Jane Austen. Her letters refer constantly to family visits which lasted for months. I have seen the Austen dwelling at Chawton. It is scarcely bigger than a dollhouse. Where Jane and Cassandra, not to speak of their parents, put up those cavalcades of relations I can't imagine. Evidently a sofa pressed into service as a sleeping place for either hostess or guest, and trundle beds beside the drawing room fire for the children, were considered matters of course when dispensing hospitality. Creature comforts did not count so much as the welcoming door.

It is not nostalgia which set me brooding on this subject but the fact that I recently spent an entire day trying to make room in our domicile for a relative coming from California for a week's stay. And I discovered something absurd—that in a family which consists for nine months of the year of only three people, and in a house with five bedrooms, however shabby, there seemed at first to be no place ready and suitable for her.

Ridiculous? Of course. But also true. Modern, privacy-hugging, object-collecting souls that we are, we had sprawled ourselves and our impedimenta over the entire three floors of this less than stately mansion.

The sunniest, the best-furnished room, complete with its own bath and television set, was automatically out of the question. That is owned by Agnes, who puts our dishes in the dishwasher and condescends to let me help her cook. I turned then to the next best, which belongs to the college daughter. It was both untenanted and newly redone. But ski poles stood in corners there, the shelves were blocked by hatboxes and hair dryers, the drawers so crammed with summer clothes and the closets so full to bursting with sheeted dresses, cartons of old composition books, and moldering but beloved tennis sneakers that there seemed no space anywhere to put up another hanger, much less a lodger. The room of her absent sister was just as cluttered, despite the fact that she lives three thousand miles away from us. Her still-cherished dollhouse took up one wall, her rows and rows of stored books the other three. And in *her* closet reposed all the random debris we persist in stowing there instead of taking properly up to the attic.

As for my husband, I couldn't expect him to move out of his cozy quarters, which were also ostensibly mine. And the hypothetical spare bedroom, a little box of a room, was the place where I invariably creep when I can't endure the arctic weather he prefers for slumber; it, too, was full of overflow from the rest of the house. I was shocked when I peeked in its bureau. But then you know what you heap up in an extra bureau if you are a squirrel like me—swatches of drapery material, evening bags, odd packages of hairpins, a half-nibbled chocolate bar, that bottle of aspirin you keep forgetting to restore to the medicine cabinet, unusable Christmas gifts, gloves without mates, dilapidated heating pads, old newspaper clippings whose reason for cutting out in the first place you have forgotten, sweaters too good to throw away but too shapeless to wear, underwear in need of mending, faded bathing suits, and unanswered correspondence. I couldn't clear the place in a month. Besides, I keep my typewriter there; I dared not be evicted.

Well, I decided, the college daughter's chaos would have to go. Bravely I uprooted skis and poles, raided her dresser, carried all her frocks away, and deposited everything in her sister's empty nest, where I could then shut neither drawer nor door. There would be lamentation when the former girl came home for vacation and found things out of order or could not find them at all. But future trouble had to wait on present necessity. I scurried about from linen closet to bedroom (the latter looking strangely bare), attempting to make it habitable for an undemanding but deserving sister-in-law. Self-indulgent I might be, unorganized and absentminded as a hostess, but I held and hold to one firm creed: that a visitor ought to be at least half as comfortable in my house as when she is at home.

Entirely easy, maybe not. If you are anything like me you never expect genuine comfort on safari. No matter where I go, I am homesick for amenities entirely personal and unimportant; I can imagine no luxury greater than the first night in my own bed after the return from a journey. Shakespeare knew about such deprivations as he knew about everything. "When I was at home, I was in a better place," says Touchstone as he wanders through Arden Forest, "but travelers must be content." Travelers must, indeed, endure what they encounter. Yet making their sojourn with us less hard than it might conceivably be is part of hospitality. And hospitality is one of the cardinal virtues.

Not that this guest would ask much. A better traveler never lived. She has inherited the triple gifts of a sweet nature, naturally curly hair, and a good digestion. Like my husband, who is her youngest brother, she thinks insomnia is a fiction and never looks askance at a gift-bed. She would have taken up residence just as happily amid the clutter I had removed as at the Plaza.

I have had visitors of a different mettle—although seldom twice. I've lodged and boarded young nieces who ate nothing but tuna fish sandwiches and who used the shower at three o'clock in the morning, and I have catered to distant cousins who hung wet handerchiefs on the backs of antique mahogany chairs. Some time ago an otherwise charming woman came to stay for the weekend. She laughed indulgently at what she called her "funny little room" (my typing cubicle), gave me her diet list, asked for her breakfast at 11 A.M., and telephoned long distance on my bill. Such behavior I could have written off as eccentricity, except for one startling antic. She came to me while I was without help of any sort in the kitchen and she came late in the day. She found me struggling at the

stove with the chicken fricassee which was, she had stipu-
lated, the one meat she could digest; and she watched m
setting up the table in the dinette for a simple meal *en*
famille. Half an hour before we were to sit down to dinne
she clutched my arm, looked me meltingly in the eye, an
asked, "Tell me, Phyllis, do we dress?"

But this expected sister-in-law of mine I truly delighte
to honor. Possibly she night not have noticed that on
whole dresser was at her disposal or that I had laid ou
for her that cake of carnation-smelling soap which fo
several weeks had been scenting my nightgowns while i
waited in a drawer for her. She would not have care
whether she got the monogrammed towels. I was takin
pains merely because I loved her and out of pride o
hospitality.

Those items arranged, I looked around to see if ther
was anything missing from hospitality's list. Ours is not
hotel, but I could take a leaf from hotel service and lear
by hotel mistakes. The lights at least were adequate. Th
sister-in-law is something of a reader, like all the famil
and would no doubt wish to do some of it in bed. Th
was taken care of already. In our household we *all* rea
in bed. In fact, my husband and I as a matter of cours
include a couple of hundred-watt light bulbs in our luggag
whenever we take to the road. We plan never again to b
trapped in an inn or a motel where, when bathed an
ready for a book in bed after our three hundred miles, w
discover that a bulb the size of an undergrown onion
all we have been provided by way of illumination. A
home we say, "Let there be light," and there is light, abo
our heads and over the left shoulder.

The bureau's cleared drawers I washed and lined with tissue paper. Next to poor lamps there is nothing so unpleasant for a visitor as to be faced with either (*a*) no drawer space at all or (*b*) drawers obviously vacated at the last minute and still retaining traces of past ownership in the way of vagrant bobby pins, stale jars of cold cream, or somebody's half-empty tube of toothpaste. Then I dropped a sachet packet into the tissue paper for the pleasure of doing it and because I collect sachets. On the dresser's top I put nothing except a pincushion holding real safety pins. If this had been summer I would have raided the garden for a bouquet, which of all decorations is the most welcoming; but it was winter, and, much as I love my relative by marriage, a flourish like hothouse flowers would have looked prententious.

The mattress, thank heaven, was sound. All hostesses, I feel, ought to be required by law to sleep now and then on the beds they offer to guests. There would be fewer aching spines in the nation. In our house we allow no sagging springs if we can help it, preferring to do without something less valuable if we must make a choice. The blankets could have been newer, but they were clean and, I hoped, sufficient. I once visited a house which owned a guest room all done up in the most expensive materials and precise colors. The bedspreads matched the curtains and the blankets matched the bedspreads. But what am I saying—*blankets?* I refer to one grudging, thin, solitary covering. It was stretched snugly over sheets with matching scalloping, and when the thermostat went down at midnight it would not have warmed a mouse. I dozed uneasily all night beneath my winter coat and one of the matching scatter rugs off the floor. Since that experience I have seen to it that my lodgers have blankets in the plural, even if I have to ravish the car of its lap robe for my own pallet.

Since this was a daughter's room by rights, there was, not unnaturally, a telephone there. I put a pencil and scratch pad near it. Even the most unassertive guest might want to jot down a note or a number. And I made sure my possessions were carted away from the desk. (I am inclined to write letters anywhere the impulse seizes me, which is seldom.) I left a usable pen and a few sheets of household stationery at hand. Ostentatious or not, that is a nice gesture.

What else might she need? Pillows? I had given her the two without which no reader-in-bed can feel snug. A chair to sit in with a lamp beside it? Yes, it was there. She's a nonsmoker, so I did not rout out my best ashtray, but I put a water glass on the bedside stand, along with a box of tissues. And I got out a luggage stand. It's a hotel touch but a useful one, as is the extra toothbrush in its plastic case which I store for emergencies in the bathroom cupboard. A toothbrush is like good health. You don't notice it much when you have it, but let it be absent and the world darkens.

As for closets, I whisked away the hangers made of wire, which I detest but which somehow sprout in such storage places like mushrooms in a lawn, and substituted stouter ones, making certain some of them were equipped with clamps for skirts. Then I tested the windows to see that they all opened or shut as the case might be and that blinds against the morning sun were in working order. (The hostess I have in my time most fervently cursed is the one who, apparently able herself to sleep with daylight full on her eyelids, provides me with no shade against the loathsome dawn.) At the last minute I emptied and lined the waste basket, that useful piece of houseware; made all as fresh and convenient as possible with my limited resources.

(Limited, that is, by our current domestic standards. When we were younger and more carefree we entertained oftener and with less ado. We also got entertained back in the same fashion. I can recall sleeping happily on army cots in half-finished weekend cottages, bedding down on sofas in small apartments, sharing daybeds and foraging for my own pillows, and giving equal treatment to guests. Now that I have more to offer, I offer it. That is hospitality's simple rule.)

With this visitor's physical comforts tentatively assured, I considered her entertainment. That was simple enough. I decided to leave her to her own devices. She had stayed with us before, and I was aware of what would please her. There had to be one evening, the first, devoted to reminiscence. She and my husband would discuss the family and her sons and daughters and *their* sons and daughters; and the two of them would debate genealogy, trying to recall whether it was Captain Daniel Spencer who fought long ago in King Philip's War or if that was Great-great-granduncle Jabez. I would make coffee for them and yawn beside the hearth. We had bought tickets for one play in the city and invited one set of friends to dinner. Otherwise her time would not be interfered with. If I knew her—and if the weather stayed reliable—she'd be off to town every morning to shop for her grandchildren, admire the new buildings, and visit every available art gallery. I am always grateful for so resourceful a guest, and I believe she is equally grateful for my lack of fuss. Certainly I bless any hostess who gives me a loose rein.

There is one house where we used to stay occasionally, but where we stay no longer, whose chatelaine issued no invitations, only orders.

"Come for a long weekend," she would write. "Reach here for dinner at seven-thirty on Friday and leave after lunch on Sunday, no later than three."

This firmly worded message was amplified when we arrived. Breakfast, we were warned, was served at nine exactly; we would all compete in croquet on Saturday morning, swim on Saturday afternoon, and play paper games on Saturday night. No shirkers who preferred bridge or conversation were asked back. Sunday we might depart so far from formula as to attend church (if we had our own means of conveyance), but before we got our luncheon we were expected to "go round the place" with the host, admiring his septic tank and commenting favorably about the grass in the east meadow. The food was good in that house and the beds were dandy. Still, we found it easier to stay at home than to live like Prussian soldiers at constant drill.

On the other hand there is a couple we visit in the country at whose house it is always Christmas of a sort. Guests are allowed to do exactly what pleases them, even to picking out the bedrooms of their choice or making themselves a sandwich from the refrigerator when they feel hungry. That they may have to scout about for their towels and sheets and wash up their own plates after the sandwich is part of the pleasure. When we go there we read, walk, talk, nap, or play cards as the mood takes us. Once a long time ago my husband summed up the delight we take there in one succinct sentence: "It's as good as being at home—plus no children."

For this is a childless couple, and when our own progeny were younger we grappled such friends to our bosoms with hoops of steel. Oh, the raptures we used to feel at waking on a summer morning to no patter of little feet and no babble of infant voices! Now that the patter and the babble have permanently departed from our echoing house, my feelings have softened on the subject. I am even willing to be amiable away from home when a five-year-old comes into my room before I'm up to show me his pull toy and ask me my age.

Still, I contend that a kind hostess tucks her infants out of the way as well as she possibly can when she entertains overnight guests. No matter how fascinating a child may seem to its own parents, no matter how beautiful or clever or full of funny sayings, visitors may prefer the conversation and company of adults. I wake with cheeks burning in the night, remembering how I used to permit mine to monopolize long-suffering guests. They weren't allowed to interrupt sleep or intrude on dinners. But I *did* let them roam at large. I *did* repeat their infant witticisms. I *did* let them show off their dancing school curtsies and display their new shoes; I wouldn't do it again if the opportunity were mine, and it would be to everyone's benefit. Children don't really want to be part of a grown-up world, but they are often prodded by unrealistic parents into thinking they do.

An artist, rather famous in his field, used to come to stay

with us. He was as patient as he was gifted, and I shudder now to recall that two little girls here used him as they would have used a paid magician—insisting that he "draw things" for them on the grimy bits of paper they pushed into his hands. When he reaches the celestial fields, I feel sure he'll receive his crown without asking for it, on particular account of this act of charity. The saddest part of the whole business is that I didn't even keep the pictures.

The sister-in-law on her way here would never have objected to hordes of children clustering about her. She is philanthropic by nature and has, besides, brought up nine of her own. Rules, however, are tested by exceptions. Her peculiar addiction to infants did not alter my basic contention. Good beds, freedom of action, no infestation of progeny—what better could a guest require?

Oh, something much better, I told myself that frosty afternoon as I completed my last duty to the room itself. To be comfortable and at ease beside an alien fireside, one needed more than a sound mattress or a well-furnished bathroom shelf. There ought to be present a true welcome.

Still, true welcomes proceed from the heart, not the mind; and hearts are difficult to instruct. In this case mine needed no instruction. This sister-in-law would be a bonus, not a burden. Perhaps, then, I thought, a welcome's temperature depended on the guest herself. The visitor who brings with her not only gifts and conversation but a disinclination for giving trouble or advice, will find hospitality flowing freely for her in any house.

But that, as Kipling used to say, is another story.

12 ✤ *What Cookbooks Don't Tell You*

Everybody who reads cherishes his own form of escape literature. It may run the gamut from comic books to Anthony Trollope, depending on what the bored vacationist or the midnight insomniac is trying to escape. Doctors devour westerns, businessmen turn to Catullus, professors relax with science fiction. I know poets who thrive on detective stories, and I am acquainted with a manufacturer who pores over the plays of Shakespeare on the train while other commuters glance at the stock-market reports. I know a witty novelist who is constant to the advice-to-the-lovelorn columns in various newspapers and magazines and a commercial artist who keeps by his bedside a copy of *First Aid to the Ailing House*, which he finds as enthralling as an Agatha Christie.

Our family, on the other hand, reads cookbooks. Many a white night I have whiled away with leafing through the directions for concocting *riz de veau jardinière* or *cornets de jambon Lucullus* or *mousse de pommes Calvados*. Actually, I have never got around to trying any of those three mouth-watering recipes. I just like to dream, and so does my husband. It isn't that we are perennially hungry or even particularly greedy. We simply find the excitement and adventure in those pages that other people do in Hemingway or John Buchan. We keep cookbooks in nearly every room in the house and can amuse ourselves by the hour, any evening, reading aloud from the spirited prose of, say, Fannie Farmer or Dione Lucas. A paragraph which begins, "Separate seven eggs and beat the whites until stiff but not dry," automatically commands our ear. There is as much music for us in the sentence, "Cut carrots in small matchsticks and onion into half slices; mix with a little salt and pepper and put in a pan with a little fat and cognac," as in a line from Keats.

We read recipes at dinner in an attempt to find out why our *coq au vin* does not taste the the same when the fowl is boned as when left stolidly vertebrate. We scurry through one culinary tome after another to track down the various versions of *bœuf Bourguignon.* We look up everything from Apples (baked) to Zabaglione. We inquire into the secrets of making potato dumplings which really remain unified balls when dropped into liquid. (The potatoes must be cooked in their jackets and mashed after being chilled, and they must contain not a drop of extra moisture.) We evoke from them the memory of dishes from our childhood or our travels. We even collect recipes for the haughtiness of their tone. My favorite among those is one set of lordly directions for assembling *crêpes Suzette.* "Take a silver skillet," it begins, as if silver skillets were everyday accouterments in any kitchen. There, if you like, is romance.

But there is one thing I have come to realize and it is that cookbooks, in their own way, *are* romances. They are not to be taken as the whole gospel. As a practicing housewife, I have often had to alter the sacred Word to my own uses. I have also found that those volumes I prize so highly are written by fallible human beings who leave out, at times, truly vital information. You can trust them to list the proper ingredients for a meat loaf or the correct instructions for breading chops. But there are all sorts of hints, clues, informational nuggets not contained in the manuals.

It used to be my ambition to write a cookbook myself, one compiled for the not-impossible Her who knew absolutely nothing about a stove, a Dutch oven, or a double boiler. I would start her from scratch.

"An egg is an object," I would tell her, "which in its natural state comes enclosed in a very brittle shell. When you wish to open one, crack it smartly in the middle across the sharp edge of some stable device, such as a thin-sided bowl. Place a saucer underneath it to catch the meat."

Or I would say, "A measuring cup is a cup with measurements written on it and preferably with a lip for pouring out. It can be made of either metal or glass. Metal ones are unbreakable, but the glass ones you can see through. When you are filling it with flour, use a spoon as a conveyer."

And so I would lead her gently along from poached eggs ("always cook them very slowly in a pan which contains water to which a little milk has been added; and break them, the eggs, into a saucer before you slide them into the pan") through boiled potatoes ("never, never put them into a pressure cooker, which turns them out mushy on the outside and like stones within") to less difficult things such as lobster Thermidore and *crème brulée.*

For I remember my own dilemmas when I was a beginner, with only a printed page to tell me how to go about this art I had neglected to acquire at my mother's knee. I recall my exasperation one day, when I was trying to bake a custard, at the author's demand that I first "caramelize the dish." I hadn't the faintest idea how one caramelized a dish, nor had the writer thought to tell me. I was forced to call up a friend of mine, a veteran of many seasons, before I could get under way with melting the sugar slowly into the right liquid and sepia consistency.

Another embittering experience was my attempt to "stir" something until "the mixture coats the spoon." How did a spoon look when coated? And was the coat supposed to be heavy, spring-weight, or diaphanous? It was a long time before I learned, and even now I find a thermometer more reliable than a fashion tip.

No book in my library has ever told me something I stumbled across by myself—that when the expert bids you "lightly brown" a slice of meat, you must first preheat the skillet to browning temperature, as you do an oven before you put in a cake, or else the veal slices or the chicken breasts will never attain the desired golden shade which gourmets praise.

"But," you will argue, "those experts expect you to have common sense."

All I can offer in rebuttal is the remark that common sense is frequently the fruit of experience and that a cook who, like me, has to learn her trade, humble and single-handed, at her own stove is often lacking in it.

It took me much trial and error to find that the only possible way of telling whether or not a steak is done is to cut into it to see, barbarous as that procedure may sound. Silver was dusting my hair before I understood how to keep parsley fresh for more than a day or two in the refrigerator.

(You wash it, I discovered, dry it well, cut off the longer stems, and put it delicately into a jar with a tight lid.) I had to experiment to learn that carrots must go into a stew at least fifteen minutes before the potatoes (if the stew is simmering, as it should, instead of boiling) and that the latter delectable vegetable can never be warmed over as it stands. Stew profits by a second day's reheating. The carrots remain carrots. The onions prosper. The meat takes on a more fervent flavor. But the potatoes at that second meal taste like lumps of old canvas, stale, flat, and unprofitable. There are a hundred splendid ways of using them again. Just don't try to serve them twenty-four hours old in their original dress.

As a matter of fact, I have a bone to pick with most modern cookbook compilers when it comes to their attitude on potatoes in general. They snub them. The fad for slimming has nudged our native American staple out of the high place it deserves to occupy on menus. A potato is as necessary to the diet as milk, contains no more calories than an orange. And for pure, lasting, day-by-day satisfaction, nothing else invented in the way of food outlasts its charms. Potatoes properly baked are a delicacy, correctly mashed (with all water drained away, the milk hot, every lump dissolved) are a treat for the nicest palate. I cannot think of ambrosia more subtle than tiny new potatoes cooked in their scrubbed jackets, peeled, and then bathed in a sauce made with butter, olive oil, lemon juice, chives, and a dash of nutmeg. Some reformer needs to come along with "Long Live the Potato!" written bright on his shield.

The books improve as years go by and cooks become less and less often initiated from childhood into kitchen mysteries. For one thing, they now have pictures, sometimes too beautiful for imitation, but frequently valuable. And now the best of them list, at the beginning of the first chapter, definitions of such basic terms as "sauté," "scald," "braise," or "marinate." They explain the functions of herbs and the importance of garlic. They spell out what is meant by "double-action baking powder." They tell you which pots to use for simmering soup, the way to differentiate "dry" bread crumbs from the "soft" variety, how to substitute cocoa for chocolate. Still, there are all sorts of fundamental information they leave out.

Do they tell you, for instance, such vital items as the Impossibility of Using Up Easter Eggs? Not at all. They instruct you how to boil the eggs; how, maybe, to dye them; even how to serve a few of them in a cream sauce on Easter Monday. What they do not warn you is that most of those lovely, varicolored objects are going to linger first in a dish on the table, then in the refrigerator, and finally like a deadweight on the conscience well into the following month. Unless you have a family who is egg-mad, there is no way at all of disposing of them short of feeding them to neighborhood cats or giving a cocktail party and passing them, stuffed, as canapés.

Nor do they caution you about the occasional spite of inanimate objects. I don't know that a scientific study has ever been made of this phenomenon. But it is a fact that once in a while kitchen tools run amok, grow malign as trolls. Some black morning every cook will come into her domain to find her slaves suddenly become foes. Knives bite the hand that wields them, cups stick to saucers, plates shatter, sinks stop up, stoves burn the pudding, toasters scorch the bread, spoons leap from the fingers, corkscrews crumble the cork in the bottle. On such a day there is no use trying to deal with such malevolence. Despite your best diplomacy, cakes will refuse to rise, meat to turn tender, vegetables to remain green or savory. The sensible policy is either to warm up yesterday's macaroni and cheese or else take the family out to dinner until the storm blows over. It is certain to pass.

Only one mischief remains constant. I call it the Theory of the Unwatched Pot or McGinley's Law. And the facts are these: You are stirring a mixture which obstinately refuses to boil, even to break its placid surface with a bubble. The phone rings. And in the instant between lifting your hand from the spoon and picking up the earpiece, the stuff not only will begin furiously to bubble like a witch's caldron, but will boil *over*, trailing its sticky spoor down the freshly cleaned stove onto the floor. Nobody has hinted at so great a truth, but there it remains—as immutable as the rule of gravity.

Another bit of information concerns Friday-night guests. I own a recipe for Fridays which tastes even more delightful than it looks and is as easy to prepare as a frozen dinner. To one pound of sole, lying gracefully in an open shallow pan (preferably one of the enameled iron pans which have added such a lot of decorative comfort to the modern kitchen), add one can of undiluted frozen cream-of-shrimp soup. Sometimes I also add embellishments—a little sherry and flour (for the sherry dilutes the soup and must be thickened, tablespoon for tablespoon), extra shrimps, pieces of lobster meat. Then I dot it all with butter, shake over it a light coating of grated Parmesan cheese, and thrust it into an oven set at 375 degrees. Half an hour later out comes the handsomest party dish you could ask for. There is only one flaw. I have seldom been able to serve it for company without discovering, too late, that there is one guest present who is allergic to shellfish.

The prevalence of such accidents ought to be pointed out to the budding hostess.

Where, too, is the genius who will openly publish something all cooks must eventually learn—that you can never taste the food at your own dinner party? No matter how artfully I have braised the chicken or contrived the asparagus hollandaise or rolled the hazelnut roll over its cream filling, all, all is dust in the mouth at eight o'clock when we sit down at my personal table. I have chewed relentlessly on ham that seemed composed entirely of cardboard, on salad with no more flavor than tissue paper, while about me the guests were cheerfully devouring what they claimed were succulent delicacies. To discover this odd development early will help many a young housewife to get through an evening without brooding.

Cookbooks do not tell you that, nor do they warn you about the eating habits of husbands. McGinley's Law has many codicils, and one of the most time-tested of them consists of the conclusion that whenever I plan something especially tempting for dinner, I am being redundant.

"Shad roe tonight, dear," I announce happily when the lord of the manor comes in the door with the evening paper under his arm.

Instead of the delighted smile, there will flit across his face a grimace of anxiety.

"Now isn't that a coincidence," he'll say, never one at

loss for the encouraging word. "It's just what I had for lunch."

It is experiences like that which unnerve beginners. They ought to be warned against such contingencies, just as they are cautioned not to overcook the calves' liver or let the onions brown, instead of merely yellow, for spaghetti sauce.

But then there are all sorts of knowledge which the texts ought to impart along with the measurements and the recipes. Young mothers ought to be told the truths of baking day, ought to be primed with the flat assertion that in a house where children live, there is no such thing as too many cookies. Make them by the dozen, by the hundred, by the crockful. Stud them with raisins, decorate them with chocolate bits, fold them full of nuts. Make them thin, fat, soft, or crunchy—however you concoct them, they will mysteriously melt away before nightfall, like a spring snow.

Indeed, a whole chapter might well be devoted to the appetites and tastes of the young. For no matter how strictly their palates have been developed, however well indoctrinated they have been by epicurean parents, they are bound to run to strange and shocking preferences in food. Ask a child of eleven which he would rather dine on—Rock Cornish game hen with wild rice and mushrooms or tuna fish and noodles—and he will invariably settle for pizza pie.

A friend of mine who is Viennese and a cook ripe for the honors of a *cordon bleu* has told me a touching story concerning her own son of about that age. His taste has been carefully educated. He is ostensibly an underage gourmet. So when his birthday came along and she was inquiring into what he wanted for a glorious anniversary menu, she was heartened but not astonished by his brief sketch of what he considered the Good Dinner.

"I'd like snails first," he said. "And then *filet mignon.* With Béarnaise sauce. And then an artichoke, maybe?"

"Yes, yes," she agreed. "That would be wonderful. And I'll steam the rice in consommé the way you like it. And then," she prompted him, "for dessert?"

"Dessert?" He deliberated for a minute or two, searching his mind for an image of the perfect sweet.

His mother's eyes were shining with anticipation, with the joys of contriving for him something really imperial, like a *Sachertorte* or cherries jubilee.

Finally he spoke. The sword fell. "*I* know what I want," he said. "Tootsie Rolls!"

I would write things like that down in my cookbook. I would not omit the accidental or the startling or the unorthodox. I would explain that canned peas and canned corn are not substitutes for fresh ones, as many people think, but entirely different kinds of food, pleasant in themselves if not too much is expected of them. I would suggest that one can easily put too much tomato into almost anything; although, on the other hand, a small amount of tomato puree is tasteless in a meat sauce and perfect for giving it the gloss and color one sees in pictures. I would harp on the exquisite flavor of that lowly and often spurned vegetable, the beet, which—when small and childish—can be as delicious as anything grown in a garden.

And I would dwell on something the texts always leave out—the sensual joy of cooking itself. For this, the most creative of all the household arts, can bring pleasure not only in the product but in the manufacture. Any good cook takes delight in seeing whites of egg foam up about the beater, light and virginal as summer clouds. She revels in the feel of dumpling batter under the just-perceptible touch of her fingertips. She likes to hear the sizzle of a fritter on the griddle, the tiny tune the ragout makes when it simmers.

Lying in bed one night, reading the evening newspaper, I found myself haunted by a kind of ache in my bones, teased by a faint desire. And I knew what it was I yearned to do. I wanted to go down into the kitchen, open the refrigerator, and lift out the enameled dish in which I was marinating a cut of beef for *Sauerbraten*, planned as dinner for the day after tomorrow. I longed to turn that dripping object over in its sweet, sour, spicy, fragrant broth, feeling the weight and substance of the meat gripped in my hands.

So pad down I did, while the house slept, to enjoy myself for a few splendid moments with my little masterpiece.

And what did I bring back to read myself to sleep with instead of the discarded paper or a mystery novel? Why, a cookbook, one I had not had time to finish before. It might not contain all gospel, but I knew it would compose me better than a tranquilizer.

13 ⸙ *Kitchens Are for Cooking*

Something earthshaking is going on at our house. The furniture is sheeted against plaster dust, and we eat our breakfasts, standing, beside a half-dismantled sink. All day long, men in overalls hammer, saw, tear out pieces of wall, lay pipes, discuss the weather, measure for linoleum, and drink coffee from Thermos bottles. We shut our ears against the astonishing noise and take our dinners out.

For at long last we are succumbing to an American mania. Our kitchen—this cozy, undistinguished, but familiar room, where I learned to cook by ear and intuition and which I had thought sufficient for my needs—is having its face stylishly lifted. There will be cabinets where windows used to let in redundant light. I shall have drawers for silverware and drawers for mixing bowls, compartments planned solely for trays, cupboards to hold more dishes than I own, and slots where knives can disappear up to their handles. I will no longer have to lug the ironing board off the back staircase where it used to stand or stretch on tiptoe to reach the nutmeg. Soap will flow from a dispenser next to the spray hose.

I'm certain I'll love it once I get used to it and learn how to manipulate all those cunning new controls and find my way around alien storage bins. But it was hard for me to accept alterations.

On friends who remarked from time to time about my valor in bringing out meals from a range purchased well before the war and with a refrigerator shamelessly unconcealed by a fretwork-decorated nook, I always turned a surprised glance.

"Out of date?" I asked. "Why? My oven still bakes. I *like* having an old laundry hamper beside the stove where the cat can sharpen her claws. I *want* a table in the middle of the floor. I'm used to it. And we eat all right, don't we?"

I resisted my husband when he complained that nobody, not even he, could any longer repair a faucet with its threads worn to the nub. I held out against our financial adviser, who hesitantly mentioned that if we ever wanted to sell this house it might be wise, it might be—umm—advisable, to modernize a little.

Then three catastrophes overtook me. I caught my heel in a piece of curling tile near the sink and went sprawling. The handle of the stove's forward burner refused to turn and no replacement could we find for it. And the dishwasher—a mere infant of a dishwasher, only twelve years old—prematurely broke down. Obviously the kitchen had to be worked on, and we might as well go the whole way. We would install custom-made cabinets. We would change the windows, buy a new stove with a hood and a fan, be nearly as fashionable as our friends. But against one improvement I set my stubborn face. I would not have an oven in the wall.

It is that incorrigibly chic fixture which has become for me the symbol of a cult I do not wish to join. I admit it is useful, practical, decorative. I also believe it stands for something I deplore—styling for styling's sake.

Do not misunderstand me. I am not against progress, certainly not against convenience. Each real step forward in improving cuisine I applaud with my whole heart. I love every useful tool the gadgeteers contrive for me, every whisk, press, cutter, grinder, chopping board, or double boiler which helps make my tasks easier and my table better endowed. I would like to award medals and annuities to those anonymous geniuses responsible for automatic beaters, thermostats, and blendors.

"Gentlemen," I often say to them in thought, "you are the props of civilization. You—the chap who dreamed up the percolator, you who invented pilot lights or paper napkins—are the true benefactors of mankind."

I remember when I first got my electric dishwasher how I used to pat its pretty little porcelain head every time I passed it, out of sheer gratitude.

But, guilelessly, I have always believed kitchens were for cooking. It alarms me when I discover they are being turned into something much less, into showpieces, status objects, like foreign sports cars or leopard coats. On the real estate market it is a truism nowadays that unless the kitchen of a house up for sale is "modern," is polychromatic, wall-ovened, freshly even if cheaply tiled, a buyer is nearly impossible to find. That the elderly room might have excellent light and an adequate stove and capacious broom closets and better storage cabinets, however old-fashioned, than any new domicile can boast, counts for nothing with prospective purchasers, Surface is all. When they complain that "It isn't efficient," they really mean, "It isn't as stylish as my neighbor's."

And what comes out of these modern offices, up to date as a Givenchy gown? Well, in too many cases it is a horrid substitute for good food—thawed meals, frozen dinners. For what concerns me most about the great kitchen fad in America is not that they are being prettified beyond the pale of common sense, but that they are in danger of falling into the hands of those I can only call the anticooks.

Anticooks are different from noncooks. Noncooks mean well, and they would maybe like to cook well. They just have no flair. Somehow, like music lovers who sing off key, they cannot carry a culinary tune. Their cakes fall. Their roasts are either overdone or dripping with gore; they scatter herbs too freely into casseroles and forget to take the garlic out of the salad it is supposed to flavor. Their sweet potatoes are adorned with marshmallows. They put dumplings straight into liquid and tomato into everything. But they take pains and spend time over their food and they appreciate other people's skill.

Anticooks, on the other hand, are against cooking on principle. I number several anticooks among my acquaintances, and I value them for many virtues. They are often splendid citizens, good wives and mothers. Gastronomically they are Philistines; worse than Philistines, Puritans, who feel there is something sinful in owning a palate or cultivating the holy art of cuisine. They are the people who, when planning a meal, ask themselves (as does a friend of mine) not, "Which vegetable is freshest and tastiest this time of year?" but only, "What shall I serve for a carbohydrate?" The frozen foods and packaged mixes which real cooks employ, but employ chiefly as props and stays in emergencies, are to the anticook a whole way of life. She shops for her meat once a month, buying perhaps expensive cuts from good markets. Then she pops everything into her inevitable freezer. I know one woman with a garden who raises her own beans and asparagus. She eats them sparingly during the summer but boxes them all into containers for the deepfreeze and dines during the winter alternately on one or the other.

"It's so reassuring," she confided to me once. "I never have to plan ahead. One night I have asparagus, the next night beans. It saves such a lot of worry."

The anticook owns calorie charts and vitamin tables and books which tell you how to make soup by adding water to something dehydrated, but she wouldn't know a *roux* from a Béchamel sauce if it fell into her lap. The day she looks forward to is the time when all food comes piped to the table from a central metropolitan kitchen—tasteless, effortless, and alike from coast to coast.

I went to call on an anticook recently. She had just finished with the ordeal we are currently undergoing, and she took me out to admire the result. It was a handsome room, I had to admit. There were ruffled curtains over the chromium sink. The color of her stove matched the wallpaper and, inevitably, her glass-faced oven was set into the wall. There were rows of attractive spice bottles in a pretty rack, copper molds, modish as Picassos, hanging from hooks. A flour sifter fitted cleverly into its designed cubbyhole, the scouring powder was hidden behind latticed doors. There were barstools and birch cupboards and a battery of cooking equipment.

"Beautiful," I murmured. "You must spend half your day here."

She was scandalized. "Half my day!" she exclaimed. "I wouldn't dream of it. I make it a point of honor never to spend more than an hour on all three meals. An hour and a half if we're having company."

As I looked about me, I saw what she meant. This was a parlor for her friends to envy, not a working kitchen. Nothing was meant for use. Out of that immaculate oven would never come a *crème brulée*, a soufflé, a loaf of homemade bread. She would shudder at the spectacle a real kitchen presents when it is in operation—a clutter of fruit rinds, piecrust shavings, egg-spotted bowls, untidy beaters, unwiped serving spoons, vegetable scrapings; the whole stove occupied with things stewing, simmering, blanching, sautéing, bubbling in pots. It would destroy her image of high fashion. I could imagine her in a fluffy housecoat, cutting peanut-butter sandwiches or pouring hot water onto instant coffee, but not with flour on her chin and batter spilt down her apron front. She owned a kitchen which architects call the "heart of the home." But it was a heart which throbbed faintly and emanated no warmth. It was a room not to live in but to get rapidly away from.

I had no quarrel with her wish to get away. If her family was nourished and satisfied, if she had urgent business elsewhere, I wished her Godspeed. The emancipation of women undoubtedly began when they could leave sink and kettle and move into what seemed to them a larger world. But then why this emphasis on show-window gadgets? Why the shelves of cookbooks unspotted by use? Decorations merely, like Victorian antimacassars. Her kitchen was one way of keeping up with whatever Joneses she might care to rival. And it is her influence on the national kitchen which I deprecate.

An extreme example of the anticook I read about in the papers a while ago. A young man was on trial in court for assaulting his wife with a blunt instrument—in this case, a quart jar of stuffed olives. He pleaded self-defense. His wife, he said, was kitchen-obsessed. All during their marriage a tug-of-war had been going on between her and her best friend as to who could boast the fanciest and most modern cooking area. Three times in five years, he testified, she had nagged him into letting her remodel theirs. Only a month before, she had bought a new sink, an expensive range, and half a dozen automatic gadgets, including one for instantly defrosting foods. When he reached home that fatal night and found her plotting to tear out part of the new cabinet section in order to install a bricked barbecue, he lost control.

"Everything went black," he confessed. "All right. I did throw that jar of olives at her. They were the only things handy. If she'd had a loaf of bread or a leg of lamb or something on the table, she wouldn't have got hurt.

"For the thing that made me maddest," he blurted, "was that all she ever fed me out of that darn kitchen was hamburgers and stuffed olives."

I didn't follow the case, but I hope they acquitted him. Although she was, as I have said, an extreme case, her kind increases yearly. It makes the struggle harder for practical and practicing cooks like me to install the sort of kitchen which meets our everyday needs.

In the past weeks I have met, at every turn, impediment

from designers who cater to anticooks. Take the matter of something trivial but vexing like my lost campaign for a soap dish.

I have been used to seeing one just above the water faucets in the sink, cradling a sensible bar of hand soap (which I need often). Now I learn that sink units no longer carry them.

"Surely everybody doesn't depend on detergents," I pleaded with the plumber. "Yes, I understand that dish makes the design less than streamlined. Who cares? When I'm cooking I get my hands dirty. I just want to wash them."

Nobody could supply me. Instead I was persuaded to put in the extra nozzle which squirts liquid soap on demand. It cost a good deal and is not any more useful than the simple metal holder which streamlining has discarded out of enthusiasm for the chic. I count that a victory for the anticook.

She had also been before me in my battle for a kitchen table. I wanted one in the center of the floor, exactly as I was accustomed to having it—an ordinary, movable, four-legged, wooden-topped stand. You might have thought I was advocating overthrowing the Union.

"The table is Out," I was told. "Look, you have your counters. If you like, we can build you a peninsula at right angles to your sink. We'll put barstools around it and you'll have your comforts without being dowdy. But no central table."

When I insisted I didn't want barstools, which bother my unreliable back, that peninsulas were too immobile, counters were too narrow for my purposes, they wrung their hands. And yet it is at my table (which stands on casters and which I can shove about the room as I care to) that I knead pastry, cut cookies, spread newspapers, dump my groceries, array my utensils, read my recipes, am able to be as expansive and sloppy as I please.

When the architect was adamant, I refused to create an ugly scene; I pretended to give in. But as soon as the last carpenter has departed, I intend to sneak my old friend back onto the floor and leave it there, out of date, battered, and useful as ever.

I've had trouble over my dishwasher, too. The old one was splendid until it perished. It opened from the top, held any number of plates, and devoured its own steam. The new models have been improved beyond convenience—at least for me. The roll-out kinds are all that are available. They may save space but are likely to make a cripple out of me permanently, since they can be packed only by someone using her spine as a cantilever. I shall have to kneel on the floor to use mine. Again, the anticook has won.

None of these defeats has been vital. It is the stove which has put me to the most trouble, and it is the designers of stoves whom the anticook has most dangerously influenced. Yet what is it ought to dominate a kitchen? A row of geraniums? An amusingly decorated breadboard? A set of copper-bottomed pots, costly as diamonds? Of course not. Only the stove really counts. Man invented fire and with it culture. He warmed himself and he cooked his food and so became better than the beasts. An inspired chef could do away with everything in his vicinity, could draw water from a well, use an orange crate to hold his tools, serve guests out of shells or from the leaves of trees in lieu of plates. But he (or she) could not function without a heating apparatus. And for too many years that article of kitchen equipment has been stylized away from utility.

I know this sounds like heresy; at best, like ingratitude. After all, you may justly point out, stoves now have the most perfectly insulated ovens, the precisest thermostats, the most charmingly colored enamels, the easiest-to-clean burners that engineers can contrive. True, and I am thankful for those favors. It is the theory of form which I assail. Stoves today are the wrong shape.

Shortly after the turn of the century, when gas and electricity came into national use, somebody made a stove which exactly answered a cook's purposes. (No, I have never cooked on one; for after all, while I antedate the *bossa nova*, I really can't recall the sinking of the *Maine*. Still, I have seen them in old houses, and they set me yearning.) They were not aesthetic. They stood on legs and were uncompromisingly black. But they owned fine, broad surfaces with at least four burners (and generally five, if you include the small one in the middle, so useful for melting butter or keeping water warm under hollandaise sauce). There was a broiler. There were often two ovens, and one was always on the right-hand side, sitting higher than the burners, on a level with one's elbow. No cook was expected to crouch, stoop, squat, or stand on her head to baste a roast. And at the back of the entire machine was the nicest feature of all—a shelf with a hood over it, where plates could hold their temperatures and gravies and vegetables keep hot. It was called a warming oven.

Then came the passion for streamlining, and the stove became what? A square box. Broiler and oven dropped lower and lower, one often built under the other, so you could not count on preparing a steak and a pudding at the same time. The warming oven disappeared. Only in the most expensive models could you find more than four burners, and even then one of those sometimes turned into a well for absentee stewing or a grill for flipping infrequent hot cakes. Anticooks loved it because it was stylish and became a good excuse for noncooking. Real cooks protested but their voices were drowned out. When finally (years later) their disapproval became loud enough to reach manufacturers, designers countered not with a better-shaped stove but with an oven separate from the rest of the equipment. In other words, the oven in the wall. It *is* an answer of sorts. It sits at a convenient height. It saves space. Below it one can build a range with as many burners as one can afford. But you can't take it with you. It is costly because it is custom-made. And it leaves the ordinary commercial stove exactly what it has been for thirty years—an inefficient box.

For our own kitchen we found our own solution. We are buying the kind of stove sold to restaurants. And you know what? It looks almost exactly like the ranges fashion discarded before the First World War. It is black. It has four legs. It owns two ovens (one at elbow height), six burners, a grill, and a warming shelf. The anticook would scorn it out of hand, and, indeed, it is not aesthetically pleasing except to me. But around it my small world will suitably evolve.

Other answers will come to other homemakers, and they may be better than mine. Perhaps they will find something more useful to them than my stove or my clumsy center

table, or the clawed hamper I am slyly bringing back t
satisfy the cat. They will be able to design a room efficien
as mine but handsomer, eliminating the makeshifts wit
which I insist on being surrounded.

But the kitchen will not come into its own again unt
it ceases to be a status symbol and becomes again a work
shop. It may be pastel. It may be ginghamed as t
curtains and shining with copper like a picture in
woman's magazine. But you and I will know it chiefly b
its fragrances and its clutter. At the back of the stove wi
sit a soup kettle, gently bubbling, one into which every da
are popped leftover bones and vegetables to make stock fo
sauces or soup for the family. Carrots and leeks will spraw
on counters, greens in a basket. There will be somethin
sweet-smelling twirling in a bowl and something savor
baking in the oven. Cabinet doors will gape ajar an
colored surfaces are likely to be littered with salt an
pepper and flour and herbs and cheesecloth and pot holde
and long-handled forks. It won't be neat. It won't eve
look efficient. But when you enter it you will feel the pul
of life throbbing from every corner. The heart of the hom
will have begun once again to beat.

14 ❧ *The Tools of the Trade*

There is an old parlor game everybody must have played from time to time on desultory evenings. The basic premise is always the same. You are cast away on a desert island. Which companion, if you could select only one, would you choose to be marooned with? Or which book? Or what single lifesaving implement?

It is a famous pastime and has elicited some famous answers. Although the preferred artifact does not vary much—it is usually a knife or an ax or a fishing rod—the other selections do.

G. K. Chesterton, in response to the query, "If you could carry only one work of literature with you, what would it be?" did not mention either Shakespeare or the Bible. He answered practically, "*The Complete Manual of Shipbuilding*."

And some anonymous woman sounded equally sagacious when the question was put to her, "Out of all the men in the world, whom would you pick for a fellow castaway?"

"That's easy," she said. "A good obstetrician."

Sometimes when I am busy in the kitchen, I play a humbler version of the game all by myself. I try to decide which of my cooking tools I would most dislike to be parted from. The stove I give myself, the way a golfer gives himself a handicap. That is so vital an object that without it nothing else would matter.

"But suppose," I say to myself, "that I was arbitrarily limited to three or four or half a dozen gadgets. Which would I choose?" Grinder, blendor, mixing bowl? Kettle, pressure cooker, roasting pan, percolator? Automatic beater, electric grill—spoon, whisk, can opener? There they sit, my slaves and minions. I love them all. But as I affectionately survey them, I wonder, had I to do without most of them, which would seem indispensable.

The answers I come up with surprise even me. For all that I value the whole array and have gone on record to attest their worth, it is usually the smallest, cheapest, most modest tools I decide to keep. Having played the game so often, I have now pretty thoroughly weeded out the list; and it might comfort some young housewife, faced with the expense of equipping a new kitchen, to listen to it. She'll have to remember, however, that when I speak of tools, I mean cooking tools per se. Robots, no matter how ingenious, which save only time or effort (like the garbage-disposal unit, like the dishwasher), do not count. The implements I choose contribute in some way to the ultimate glory of cuisine.

High on my list of necessary inventions, for instance comes something as simple as a garlic press. It is small, it is inexpensive, it is unautomated. Yet I would sooner give up a dozen fancier objects. In our household we are devoted to the flavor of garlic, but to the flavor only. We do not wish to find that stalwart herb half-cooked in a stew or raw and overlooked in a salad bowl, as I once did at a luncheon party. I swallowed it that time, in mistake for a bit of cucumber; and for days afterwards I walked alone. Mobs dispersed where I came, strong men fell back swooning, in elevators I was never jostled. So when I use garlic myself, I am wary, wanting only the faint persuasive tang of it cooked happily into a dish. I slice my bean, I press it through my little gadget, and when the casserole or the ragout it is destined to embellish is done, nothing remains but the presence of grace. If I were counseling a bride, I would beg her to forgo, if she had to, the beautiful and costly pans, the elaborate machines, the seldom-used chafing dish. "Get yourself a garlic press first," I would say. "The rest can come in time."

Then I would add, considering, "While you're at it, be sure to buy a rubber spatula, too."

You know the kind I mean. You can get them in any hardware store for the price of an ice-cream soda—a blunt half-moon of rubber fixed to a wooden handle. I would be desolate if I had to stir a cake, fold egg whites into anything, unfold batter, scrape out a bowl without it. During the war they were unobtainable except in ersatz rubber, about as pliable as oak, and I grieved for mine. Stoically and without complaint I put up with other lacks. I used honey in lieu of sugar, learned how to make sour cream do in place of butter, lived largely on Spam for one eerie month in the country. Still, I felt hostilities were over only when a neighbor rushed in the back door one morning with a whoop of triumph.

"Guess what I got hold of just now! One for you and one for me. We're at *peace!*"

And she handed me my rubber spatula.

But then almost all the finest inventions are simple ones. Think how much more useful are paper napkins than atom bombs, matches rather than airplanes. On the same principle I prefer my pepper mill to an electric oven and my lettuce basket to the grill which automatically rotates my trussed chicken. My own pepper grinder is enormous, designed probably for outdoor barbecues. But I keep it devoutly on a counter next to the stove, ready to flake peppercorns, the spice of kings, into the dish they deserve. That I would lug along with me on any trek.

And although I could probably dry salad greens perfectly well by the method my mother used—spreading them on tea cloths until every drop of moisture had vanished—the lettuce basket made of wire is more efficient. It hangs half the day from a knob over my sink, filled with lettuces or endives or watercress waiting to be stored in the refrigerator. I would mourn it.

What else do I love most dearly? Well, there's the little pastry brush I keep for spreading egg whites lightly on tops of pies to brown them, for brushing fowl, for dusting powdered sugar over desserts. There is the pastry cutter, too, which gives you a scientific advantage in mixing piecrust, biscuits, dumplings. With it, your warm hands need never touch the shortening and so toughen the dough. I cherish the sharp scissors I keep at hand in a drawer, ready for a dozen uses. I snip parsley with them, trim crusts, cut mushrooms in halves, dice celery, brandish them in many cases more deftly than a knife. There is my colander, vital as pot or pan. How, without it, could I satisfactorily drain vegetables, steam rice, lift soup meat out of the kettle?

There are the flat wooden boards I use on either side

of my sink. I have particular fondness for them since they are an invention of my own. My husband made them for me out of good, hard wood which does not easily warp; unvarnished so that they can be scrubbed white like old tables. They span the counters and protect those colored surfaces which it seems almost sacrilege to scar with chopping and cutting. They are also movable, of course. When I am done with shaping large carrots into little ones, or with dicing celery or onion or cabbage, I slide the board toward me over the counter's edge and, with one movement of my hand, sweep the vegetables onto a plate held under it. Nothing falls on the floor to be trod on. No bits and pieces are left unused.

Those boards I would miss.

I must confess there are certain cherished tools of mine which I scarcely dare advise; for they are next to impossible to find in the stores. A long-handled three-tined fork is one. You can buy any number of *two*-tined forks but seldom one with the useful three prongs. My trident is an heirloom, and, look as I will, I cannot discover a new one to replace it when, as must inevitably happen, the handle wears away or the tines dissolve with age and use. If you are lucky enough to come across one, possess it at once. Nothing could be better for testing the doneness of foods, for lifting roasts out of the oven, turning bacon, handling any sort of bulky vegetable. I employ it in tandem with another favorite implement, the long-handled wooden spoon, which is so much gentler than a metal one when you do not wish to bruise fish or fowl. No well-appointed kitchen ought to lack that, either; nor does it need to, since the wooden spoon is happily available.

The other undiscoverable item, however, is an old-fashioned steamer. I know how hard it is to procure, for I spent several frustrating weeks not long ago trying to locate one.

No, I don't mean a clam steamer or a corn steamer. Those I was blithely shown when I inquired at my pet department store, one which specializes in kitchen goods. I refer to an apparatus designed particularly for cooking dumplings—apple dumplings, cranberry dumplings, mincemeat dumplings, especially the biscuitlike dumplings so luscious with lamb stew or chicken fricassee. We always owned one when I was a child, and I recall that it consisted of a lidded pot fitted with small cups rather like egg poachers, except that those cups were perforated. They sat in a rack well above the waterline in the pot. Into them you dropped your batter, turned up your heat, clapped on the lid, forbore to peek even once, and when in twenty minutes you lifted them out, there were the dumplings—airy, delicious, food for gods.

Does no one demand dumplings with stew any more? I am beginning to think not, since the essential vessel for their manufacture has apparently disappeared. If so, something wonderful has vanished from our tables. Yet dumplings are as easy to make as—well, as easy as pie, which they halfway resemble. You must know the kind I mean. You whip them up in five minutes from flour, baking powder, milk, a bit of butter, an egg; to that basic recipe *I* add chopped parsley and a pinch of nutmeg. The far-from-secret ingredient for the lightest imaginable tidbits of that sort is not really an ingredient but a method. *They must never touch liquid while they cook.* In lieu of a steamer, I place them carefully on top of the meat and vegetables in my stew. The drawback there is that one never knows exactly how long to cook the meat beforehand so that the twenty minutes' extra steaming will not overdo the whole dish.

Finally, after experimenting vainly with strainers and colanders, I found a device which works. It turned up at a Hungarian food shop, and consists of a simple slotted basket fitted with expanable legs. I place it into a deep pot, spoon the batter onto its buttered surface, and although the dumplings do not emerge all the same size and shape, as they do from cups, their texture and taste is the same I remember from childhood. The apparatus cost me $1.78, but I guard it like the Koh-i-noor diamond.

So far I have mentioned only contrivances which lift or cut or brush or prepare foods. What about the cooking vessels themselves? Which of my charming, hard-earned pots and pans and roasters and double boilers would I keep with me were I permitted only one or two? I do not have to think twice. All of them I treasure, but I would point without hesitation to the black iron Dutch oven and the heavy, back-breaking iron skillets, which of all my tools I use the most. I bought them twenty-five years ago at a special sale during the splendid days of the Great Depression. Four frying pans of various sizes *and* the Dutch oven cost me two dollars. I would fight for them like a tiger. In the pot I simmer everything which must cook for a long time, like pot roast, *pot-au-feu*, *Sauerbraten*, soup, spaghetti sauce. It is unbreakable, unchippable, heavy-lidded. It holds, spreads, and diffuses heat. The skillets have the same virtues, and all of them can be used on top of the stove or in the oven. They have no beauty, but they serve me perfectly and will outlast me. Peasant implements, no doubt; but like fire and water and herbs, they are cookery's great gifts.

None of my favorite gadgets, as you see, are expensive. Basic tools seldom are.

I can think of several other unextravagant aids and comforts to the cook which may not be vital, like the ones I have listed, but are nice to have on hand. I would miss my flour sifter, of course, and a good set of measuring spoons and cups. I would dislike to be separated from a wire whisk for beating eggs less brutally than does a rotary beater or an automatic one; and I find many uses for large pieces of cheesecloth. How do you keep fresh salmon whole without cheesecloth for lifting it? Or to make a *bouquet garni?*

And naturally I value my knives—my knives with serrated edges for slicing loaves, cold meats, anything solid; my sharp, sharp paring knives, honed twice a month. I admire the pliable little knife I keep for cutting grapefruit and orange sections, and the slender-bladed tool for carving fowl. If I could have only one, I would keep the last, since in a pinch it would cut everything from onions to roast turkey.

I like my opener which clamps on tight-closed lids and with a twist brings them free. I am fond of my mallet for pounding meats like scallopini of veal, Swiss steaks, and the like; although one could always make do with a heavy saucer. I enjoy my ladles and my slotted spoons for lifting vegetables out of their broth without wasting it. And I love my gigantic soup kettle. Years ago I bought it over my husband's protests. It holds I-don't-know-how-many gallons, and he was sure we would never fill it. But all winter long it is in use. The considerate butcher saves me fine marrow bones and veal knuckles and picks out shins of beef for me; and at least once a month we feast on soup so nourishing and flavorsome that one sniffs it like a garden and makes a whole dinner from it. Yet if I had to dispense with the kettle I could still make soup in my iron Dutch oven out of any leftover bones and vegetables I happened to have around.

Coffee-making would give me pause if I had to choose a vessel for it. Our kitchen owns an electric percolator which is as intelligent as a dolphin, making the coffee, turning it off, keeping it warm for any desired time. I am devoted to it. But if it were to be taken away, I could still brew coffee in an ordinary pot, clarify it with eggshells, and I think we would be satisfied with our drink. You see my point, I hope. The adorable gadgets which delight our lives are chiefly savers of labor, luxuries. I am as fond of luxuries as the next woman, perhaps a little fonder. But when making up my lists of the absolutely essential, they always go first.

There is only one slave for which I would weep salt tears were I to be suddenly deprived of it. That is my automatic blendor.

The blendor, to my mind, is an appliance not yet fully appreciated in kitchen circles. Although no bride considers her gift display complete without one, it later is apt to sit idly on a shelf, used only occasionally for making party drinks or milk shakes. It is considered a toy, like an ice crusher. I, on the contrary, think of it as my right-hand assistant. It occupies the most accessible corner of my kitchen, and its humming delights my ears continually at meal-getting time. Do I want to thicken a sauce, purée a vegetable, plan a cream soup, chop nuts, prepare a *pâté?* The blendor does my work for me. Before it was invented I used to spend hours making vichyssoise when I wanted to show off for company—pressing leeks and potatoes through cheesecloth and a sieve. Now, once they have been well simmered in chicken broth, I dump them into my amiable machine, and out they come, ground to perfection, ready to be stirred into the cream. Leftover vegetables are no longer a weight on my conscience while they dry up in the refrigerator. I add them to stock, slice in a bit of onion, put in a spoonful of flour and a cup or two of milk, drop in the butter or the parsley, stir them in the blendor—and I have a luncheon soup or a first course at dinner.

Have you tried a blendor for making bread stuffings? It whirls your bread into soft crumbs in a moment. It shreds cheese for au gratin dishes. It takes lumps out of sauces, gravies, *roux.* It makes a foolproof hollandaise sauce, an excellent Béarnaise. It is splendid for mayonnaise.

And with molded desserts it has a special cunning. One of the favorites of our table is a peach mousse, concocted in ten minutes at most. I dissolve a package of orange gelatin into a cup of hot canned-peach juice. To that I add one cup of drained peaches, a quarter of a cup of port wine or Marsala, and put the whole thing into the blendor, solidly capping it with the lid. After the ingredients have been well whipped, I add a quarter pint of heavy cream and let the mixture twirl for a mere five seconds. (You know what happens to cream if it is beaten too long; you wouldn't want butter in your mousse.) I pour it all into a melon mold and refrigerate it for half a day. If you wish to adorn your dish, drape around the mousse a generous helping of fresh or frozen peaches before it comes to dinner.

Yes, if in playing the game I allow myself electricity on my desert island, it is the blendor which heads my list of necessary automations.

Your choices will not be the same as mine. After all, it is difference which gives opinion its spice. But try the amusement for yourself sometime. I think you will discover what I have—that it is the simplest, most fundamental tools you will use most often and value highest. I love having an army of conveniences, and so does every housewife. But the beginner does not need to despair if she can afford only a few. Let her take herself to a kitchenware department, provide herself with the basic iron vessels, the little inexpensive aids, and she can learn to become as skilled a chef as if she had spent a fortune. The Day of the Robot is not yet wholly here.

15 • *The Myth of Grandmother's Cooking*

One of the American legends which takes longest to die is the story of Grandmother's prowess at the stove. (If you are young enough, perhaps it is Great-grandmother you boast about.)

Aproned, rosy, floured to the elbow, that gifted figure haunts the folkways of memory, serving up prodigious meals beside which our poor modern efforts seem meager and uninspired.

Ah, we sigh, her apple dumplings! Her fried chicken! Her popovers and gingerbread and rice fritters! Oh, the cool, mysterious cellars from which she fetched up the pickles, the jellies, the mincemeat, the preserved fruit—all done by her own hands, and all ambrosia! Ah, the slabs of devil's food cake she handed us on flowered plates to munch with milk on August afternoons! Nobody nowadays, we insist, has skill or patience—or the secret and forgotten recipes—to compete with her.

Like most myths, the tale possesses just a faint core of validity. That Grandmother often had talent, I admit. That she set as good a table as we do now, I stoutly deny. My contention is that any housewife today, provided she is not impoverished, illiterate, or unconquerably indifferent to the pleasures of the palate, can contrive better dishes than Grandmother ever imagined.

The revelation dawned on me some twenty years ago, when a favorite great-aunt came to pay me a visit. Great-aunt Johanna was an elderly widow who had recently sold her house and was preparing to move West to be near her married son. I urged her to stay with me and my family for a few months first, to recover from the wrench of leaving home. The welcome I gave her was real and warm. Not only did I feel a close affection for her, but I knew her notable reputation in the kitchen and had, as a child, enjoyed her famous table. I planned to be her apprentice.

And what did I discover? That kind, good, clever Great-aunt Johanna cooked no better than I, the novice—that I had, in fact, outgrown her. What I remembered about the feasts she had once served me was like one's recollection of great houses visited at eight or nine. Seen through the disenchanted eyes of the grown-up, they always shrink in size and grandeur. Just so had Aunt Johanna's genius diminished to ordinary proportions. Her meals were ample enough, far more ample than we were accustomed to. She could concoct a smooth boiled dressing for fruit salads, roast a holiday goose, bake delicious, if somewhat yeasty, Parkerhouse rolls. At Christmastime (while the house fogged with steam and I wore out my hands helping her cut up suet and citron) she made dozens of plum puddings for us and her friends, and those had the true flavor. But for day-in, day-out culinary expression, I, like most of my contemporaries, had the edge on her.

She overboiled the asparagus, ruined the spinach by dousing it in half a saucepan of water, broiled the lamb chops—when she did not insist on frying them—to a state of dark-brown inanity. To her, a sauce meant something invariably made with milk, in which she was likely to envelop young peas, or a heavily floured lemon custard for desserts. She had never heard of a *roux,* and to her the idea of "reducing" a gravy instead of thickening it was heresy. She despised garlic, merely giving a ladylike sniff of disbelief when I quoted to her the immortal words of the French chef Marcel Boulestin: "It is not really an exaggeration to say that peace and happiness begin, geographically, where garlic is used in cooking."

A stew, to Aunt Johanna, was Monday washday fare, not a party dish. And when she condescended to make one, she put the meat into water instead of stock and boiled it to rags. Wine was something called port which gentlemen drank after dinner. Or it was something else called sherry which you offered to guests on special occasions, accompanied by tiny sweet wafers. To pour half a bottle of Burgundy over a casserole of beef seemed to her the height of frivolity. My prodigal use of shallots, of rosemary and basil, of leeks and sweet butter appalled her, just as her cooked-to-death young cabbage (in our opinion, a food for gourmets when properly simmered with almost no water and seasoned with caraway seeds) discouraged *me.* As for pastry, her cakes turned out no better than mine, her piecrust was less consistently successful.

It was while she was making a pie, in fact, that enlightenment arrived and I realized why the dear woman, once so enthroned in my heart as Empress of the Kitchen, now seemed outdated and deposed.

She stood at the table, crumbling the shortening and the

flour together haphazardly in a bowl, kneading all together with her capable fingers.

"Wouldn't you rather use a pastry cutter?" I inquired. "It's there in the left-hand drawer."

"A pastry cutter!" She looked as startled as if I had suggested that she add a touch of arsenic to the dough. "What in the world's that?"

When I showed her the little tool, explaining that with it one need not touch a warm hand to the mixture, she shook her head in pity at my foolishness.

"Child," she said, "you have your ways, I have mine. I've been making pastry for fifty years and why would I need a gadget like that? I can see and I can feel and that's enough."

Tactfully I put away the cutter and with it the recipe which had stood me in such good stead—with which I had taught myself, my friends, and my sporadic kitchen help to turn out foolproof piecrust.

We had, indeed, our private ways. Great-aunt Johanna belonged to an era with different standards, inflexible techniques. Her cooking had been a craft, never a science. Natively she was more accomplished, certainly a good deal more industrious, than I. But the American table has improved since she was a young housewife.

To begin with, we are all less provincial today in our tastes. Great-aunt Johanna, our grandmothers and great-grandmothers did certain regional dishes superbly well. If they lived in New England they were learned in the mysteries of fish chowder and blueberry pie. If the South was their milieu, they were adepts at hot biscuits and baked ham. Each environment had its specialty; even the pioneers of the western prairies knew how to fry a rainbow trout or roast a quail to perfection.

But we are inheritors of a larger legacy. We have learned from the French, the Germans, the Scandinavians, the Slavs, the Chinese. We know herbs, understand the uses of wine, are accustomed to foreign cheeses. Italians have taught us how to cook vegetables—how, for instance, to cut green beans into two long strips, drop them into the minimum of furiously boiling water, and bring them in fifteen minutes to a texture that is neither underdone nor flabby but crisply delectable. The Swedes have given us their *smörgåsbord.* The French have tutored us in fifty different arts. From them we have learned about sauces and *pot-au-feu* and puff pastes, that roast lamb should be pink in the center, and that mushrooms should remain unpeeled. In restaurants or on our travels we have eaten borsch and scallopini and *torte* and pashka and crab-meat *chasseur*, and can now whip them up ourselves. We have ceased to be a provincial nation and have both adopted and adapted the cuisines of twenty countries. The simplest cookbook now lists dozens of alien recipes which Grandmother's tome ignored.

In addition to being more knowing about food, we have also at hand a vaster variety. Grandmother had her summer fruits, her homegrown vegetables, her rows of kitchen-canned delicacies stowed away in Mason jars. But where she could keep only carrots and turnips and potatoes or possibly cabbages fresh in her cellar, we, for twelve months, see the markets tempting us with the loot of the continent. We can get strawberries in February, asparagus in March, peas in April, oranges all the year around—

can buy, at any time, broccoli, dill in the leaf, lettuce green and firm, ripe tomatoes, mushrooms, artichokes—sometimes at no greater price than we pay in their local season. Refrigeration and the airplane have changed our eating habits. Even deep-freezing, which the dedicated cook affects to despise, has added a new dimension to our tables. Frozen peas, for example, are not fresh peas. But when cooked without water in a covered iron skillet, packed below and above with leaf lettuce, flavored with butter, pressed garlic, onion juice, and rosemary, they are still an epicurean dish and certainly superior to the coleslaw and pickled beets which Grandmother depended on to give a bit of spice and color to dinner on a winter evening.

On our shelves sit the rows of concentrated beef or chicken broth which form so satisfactory a stock for casseroles, stews, sauces. Homemade stock is maybe better, but even Grandmother did not have it constantly at hand. We have discovered wild rice and water chestnuts, fennel and saffron and sour cream. Lemons are always with us. All our eggs are fresh. Nor is the cost of such tidbits prohibitive for the ordinary family. I came across a curious bit of information the other day which made the cost of living in this mid-century seem less cruel than I had supposed.

I was leafing through the 1903 edition of the standard household dictionary of that period, *The Boston Cook Book*, edited at the time by Mary J. Lincoln.

"Never buy eggs," Mrs. Lincoln warned her pupils, "about the freshness of which you have any doubt, *not even in winter*. One can easily judge which is the better economy—to pay thirty cents a dozen and find none of them full and fresh and perhaps half of them really rotten; or to pay fifty cents and obtain them . . . sound and good."

But fifty cents! I thought, in awe. And that in a time when a dollar a day was good wages for a working man and one could rent an excellent house for twenty-five or thirty a month!

The current price of eggs in New York City ranges from some forty-nine cents a dozen for small eggs to around seventy-eight for what are called the jumbo size. (I never buy jumbo eggs. They sound like something laid by the Great Auk.) Considering the extravagance of their price in 1903, I realized that another fiction had been exploded. It is a myth that Grandmother had in her larder a wealth of eggs and cream and butter and sweet milk. Unless she lived on a very prosperous farm, she had to use such luxuries much more sparingly than we if she was to keep within a moderate budget.

Nor could she trust her staples. They did not come mass-produced as they do today. Baking powder before 1900 often arrived in the kitchen in small cakes and had to be crumbled before being measured or used. Flour varied in quality, and a young cook was forced to shop about among various brands before she was able to find the sort she could rely on; and then she had to buy it, usually, in hundred-pound barrels. Cake flour was unknown. Vanilla was usually displayed in the stick. The coffee arrived unground and sometimes unroasted. Our age sometimes seems to me, remembering turn-of-the-century inconveniences, like something dreamed up by Jules Verne.

For more important than the richness and variety of our foodstuffs, or than an increase in our living standards and our knowledge of the world beyond these American shores, is the effect on modern cooking of our modern tools.

Great-aunt Johanna visited me some twenty years ago,

having since departed for a more flowery country, where she is now probably sugaring nectar-flavored puddings for the cherubim. Her reign in the kitchen began, then, in the latter part of the last century, when life, if statelier, was by today's standards almost completely lacking in domestic automation. Remember, there were no motorcars then, no airplanes. The wireless was scarcely a gleam in Marconi's eye. The vacuum sweeper had not yet displaced the broom. And in tune with the times was Great-aunt Johanna's stove. It was fueled by neither electricity nor gas but simple wood or coal. There it loomed in her kitchen, a vast black range which one shook sternly down at night and shook firmly up again in the morning.

There were no dials to twist, no controls to hold the heat steady at 400 degrees for, say, baked potatoes, or a gentle 325 for something made with eggs. It *could* be controlled by a talented commander but at great cost in watchfulness and patience. One tested the oven's temperature by hand. Even my mother, I recall, before she baked a cake always made first what she called a "try-cake"—a sample of batter baked ahead of time to determine if all was well with mixture and oven. As a child I thought it a pleasant way she had of giving me a midmorning treat, for the try-cake was usually mine to enjoy. Now I realize it was a holdover from the era of the coal stove. No wonder that, with so inconstant a kiln at her service, the woman who could bring out of it a feather-light soufflé or an imperturbable sponge cake held a high place in the neighborhood regard.

Some tools were, of course, available. The egg whisk had recently given place to the rotary beater. There were re-frigerators of a sort for which one bought ice by the pound in summertime. There were molds and patented gelatins and long three-tined turning forks and commodious soup ladles. But most of our equipment was still undreamed of. Grandmother toasted her bread over the open flame of a stove or a grate. There were no measuring tools such as we know, and one had to depend on ordinary kitchen cups and spoons. I quote from Mrs. Lincoln's instructions on how to measure half a cupful of any liquid:

"Half a cupful," she said impressively, "is *not* half the distance from the bottom to the rim. Most cups are smaller at the bottom, for which allowance must be made. Take two cups of the same size and shape, fill one with water, then pour the water without spilling, into the other cup until it stands at the same level in both cups."

My head spins, reading her. The cook forced to waste her hours measuring in such fashion every time she wanted to contrive a dessert would have accomplished little in a morning. She *had* to learn to measure by eye and ear and sixth sense. If she was gifted by nature, she learned to do it well. If she owned no aptitude, she remained forever inadequate. I have a strong belief that it was the prevalence of bad cooks in that day which made the talent of the good ones so universally renowned.

Meat thermometers did not exist, nor did meters for gauging the temperature of icings and custards. When Grandmother frosted a cake, she had to test the doneness of the sugar mixture by dropping a sample of it into cold water, where it either did or did not "form a ball." "Hard crack" and "soft crack" were familiar terms. Ordinary also was the sentence, "Take a pinch of salt," and the phrase, "butter the size of an egg." Butter like ours, square and exact in the pound, which comes wrapped in paper on which each tablespoon's worth is written out in bold, black type, would have sent Grandmother into unbelieving rapture. She was simply not used to such work-saving luxuries.

Mrs. Lincoln's recipe for snow pudding delights me by its abrupt and humane statement concerning how long to beat the eggs and gelatin.

"Beat until stiff enough to hold its shape," she advises, "or as long as your strength will allow."

Without electric beaters, blendors, or skillets; lacking our serene and obedient ovens, our automatic broilers, bakers, presses, ice crackers, waffle irons, freezers; unaware that there could exist such things as measuring cups, precise spoons and quarter-spoons, or even our laboratory-tested recipes—Grandmother accomplished miracles. The wonder is not that her cooking fell behind ours but that she managed as well as she did.

I am reminded of my own advantages whenever I make something which sounds complicated, like cream puffs or hollandaise sauce or a nut roll. Nut roll was the dessert on which Great-aunt Johanna literally based her reputation. I remember as a child how we looked forward to being given a taste of it once or twice a year after a party. It was never a very large taste, for the nut roll had to stretch. It was a delicacy requiring too much labor and exactitude to be wasted on children. It is ironic that I can now make it in not much more than half an hour and with little fear of failure, simply by virtue of the tools I own.

The recipe calls for six eggs, with the yolks and whites beaten separately; for three-quarters of a cup of sugar, a teaspoon of baking powder, a few grains of salt, and a cup and a half of pulverized walnut meats (or of pecans or hazelnuts, the last being my preference). One must also have on hand a cup and a half of heavy cream and vanilla or rum for flavoring it. Think of the labor involved in preparing those ingredients in 1900! Aunt Johanna had first to shell the nuts, then chop them with a knife and afterwards crush them underneath a rolling pin. The eggs she had to beat by hand. She had no waxed paper with which to line the pan, as I do; and her oven could not be accurately set at 325—or the 300 I sometimes use. When the roll was baked, she had still to beat up the cream and sugar with which to fill it. All told, it was a morning's work.

But I buy the nuts already shelled, pop them into my blendor, and out they come, ready to substitute for flour in the cake. My eggs go into the mixer, the whites first, then the yolks; are deftly blended with the sugar; and in a matter of minutes they emerge, frothy or creamy as required, without my having done more than attach the cord and press a button. The oven takes care of the baking, so long as I set it correctly and watch the clock. Again, when I am ready to roll the pastry, I whip the cream in the beater which arranged my eggs. I scarcely deserve credit for success.

Which brings me back to the core of my argument—that there is no excuse these days for setting a bad table. Only ignorance or sloth could account for so egregious a feat. Ignorance and sloth, of course, abound always. There are no doubt families from Maine to Arizona who still thrive on greasy meat, overcooked vegetables, cast-iron pastries. But for the housewife whose heart is warm and whose palate is educated, and whose purse is not too lean, the door to high cuisine swings wide open. She has hundreds of excellent cookbooks to consult, and the magazines monthly print new recipes. At the grocer's, the butcher's, sit the world's fruits and meats at a price she can afford. Her stove is accurate. Her tools make the labor easy. All she has to do is to follow directions. Experience still helps, as it does in every trade; so does a clear head. Neither is any longer so vital. The bride of three months ought to be able without agony to broil a chicken, stir a gravy which is lump-free and nicely browned, bring asparagus to the table with its head intact, toss a salad, and design a chocolate sauce for the ice cream.

The dinner, in fact, might well be tastier than Grandmother's, with one important and pitiful exception—the ice cream.

A three months' bride will have no apologies for it, since she has never known anything better. Gelatin and milk frozen to the consistency and flavor of cement is to her an edible treat. But I remember something a world removed from it, something so delicious that the mouth waters and the heart constricts to think of it. Grandmother made it on summer Sundays, with the help of the entire family. Into it went real cream, rich as Paul Getty, heavy as a bad conscience; eggs, sugar, fresh fruit. The custard, cooled, filled a gallon container equipped with dasher, lid, and a handle with which to agitate the mixture into glorious stiffness. That, again, fitted into a wooden bucket loaded with ice and rock salt. It was the whole duty (and pleasure) of children to turn that handle until strength could do no more. Round and round it went, on thousands of shady back porches, the sound of its Sabbath whirring as universal as the preacher's sermon and far more seductive. When young arms failed, Grandfather took over for the final revolutions.

Then the top was unscrewed, the dasher lifted out, dripping with honeydew—with something creamy, luscious, caloric, and superb—and handed to the underage laborers to lick clean. The family finished the gallon for midday dinner.

Remembering what ice cream can be, I realize there is something, after all, to the myth I have been at such pains to demolish. Until America's first, greatest contribution to gastronomic delights comes into its own again and the freezer turns once more across the nation, Grandmother's title will not really fall.

THE FAMILY

16 • *Are Children People?*

The problem of how to live with children isn't as new as you might think. Centuries before the advent of Dr. Spock or the PTA, philosophers debated the juvenile question, not always with compassion. There's a quotation from one of the antique sages floating around in what passes for my mind which, for pure cynicism, could set a Montaigne or a Mort Sahl back on his heels.

"Why," asks a disciple, "are we so devoted to our grandchildren?"

And the graybeard answers, "Because it is easy to love the enemies of one's enemies."

Philosopher he may have been but I doubt his parental certification. Any parent with a spark of natural feeling knows that children aren't our enemies. On the other hand, if we're sensible we are aware that they aren't really our friends, either. How can they be, when they belong to a totally different race?

Children admittedly are human beings, equipped with such human paraphernalia as appetites, whims, intelligence, and even hearts, but any resemblance between them and people is purely coincidental. The two nations, child and grown-up, don't behave alike or think alike or even see with the same eyes.

Take that matter of seeing, for example. An adult looks

in the mirror and notices what? A familiar face, a figure currently overweight, maybe, but well-known and resignedly accepted; two arms, two legs, an entity. A child can stare into the looking glass for minutes at a time and see only the bone buttons on a snowsuit or a pair of red shoes.

Shoes, in fact, are the first personal belongings a child really looks at in an objective sense. There they are to adore—visible, shiny, round-toed ornamental extensions of himself. He can observe them in that mirror or he can look down from his small height to admire them. They are real to him, unlike his eyes or his elbows. That is why, for a child, getting a pair of new shoes is like having a birthday. When my daughters were little they invariably took just-acquired slippers to bed with them for a few nights, the way they'd take a cuddle toy or smuggle in a puppy.

Do people sleep with their shoes? Of course not. Nor do they lift them up reverently to be fondled, a gesture children offer even to perfect strangers in department stores. I used to think that a child's life was lived from new shoe to new shoe, as an adult lives for love or payday or a vacation.

Children, though, aren't consistent about their fetish. By the time they have learned to tie their own laces, they have lapsed into an opposite phase. They start to discard shoes entirely. Boys, being natural reactionaries, cling longer than girls to their first loves, but girls begin the discalced stage at twelve or thirteen—and it goes on interminably. Their closets may bulge with footwear, with everything from dubious sneakers to wisps of silver kid, while most of the time the girls themselves go unshod. I am in error, too, when I speak of shoes as reposing in closets. They don't. They lie abandoned under sofas, upside down beside the television set, rain-drenched on verandas. Guests in formal drawing rooms are confronted by them and climbers on stairways imperiled. When the phase ends, I can't tell you, but I think only with premature senescence.

My younger daughter, then a withered crone of almost twenty, once held the odd distinction of being the only girl on record to get her foot stabbed by a rusty nail at a Yale prom. She was, of course, doing the Twist barefoot, but even so the accident seems unlikely. You can't convince me it could happen to an adult.

No, children don't look at things in the same light as people. Nor do they hear with our ears, either. Ask a child a question and he has an invariable answer: "What?" (Though now and then he alters it to "Why?")

Or send one on a household errand and you will know that he—or she—is incapable of taking in a simple adult remark. I once asked an otherwise normal little girl to bring me the scissors from the kitchen drawer, and she returned, after a mysterious absence of fifteen minutes, lugging the extension hose out of the garage. Yet the young can hear brownies baking in the oven two blocks away from home or the faintest whisper of parents attempting to tell each other secrets behind closed doors.

They can also understand the language of babies, the most esoteric on earth. Our younger child babbled steadily from the age of nine months on, although not for a long while in an intelligible tongue. Yet her sister, two years older, could translate for us every time.

"That lady's bracelet—Patsy wishes she could have it,"

the interpreter would tell me; and I had the wit hastily to lift my visitor's arm out of danger.

Or I would be instructed, "She'd like to pat the kitten now."

We used occasionally to regret their sibling fluency of communication. Once we entertained at Sunday dinner a portrait painter known rather widely for his frequent and publicized love affairs. He quite looked the part, too, being so tall and lean and rakish, with such a predatory moustache and so formidable a smile, that my husband suggested it was a case of art imitating nature.

The two small girls had never met him, and when the baby saw him for the first time she turned tail and fled upstairs.

The older, a gracious four, came back into the living room after a short consultation, to apologize for her sister's behavior. "You see," she told him winningly, "Patsy thinks you're a wolf."

It was impossible to explain that they had somehow confused the moustache and the smile with a description of Little Red Riding Hood's arch foe and were not referring to his private life. We let it pass. I often thought, however, that it was a pity the older girl's pentecostal gifts did not outlast kindergarten. She would have been a great help to the United Nations.

Young mothers have to study such talents and revise their methods of child rearing accordingly. To attempt to treat the young like grown-ups is always a mistake.

Do people, at least those outside of institutions, drop lighted matches into wastebaskets just to see what will happen? Do they tramp through puddles on purpose? Or prefer hot dogs or jelly-and-mashed-banana sandwiches to lobster Thermidor? Or, far from gagging on the abysmal inanities of *Raggedy Ann,* beg to have it read to them every evening for three months?

Indeed, the reading habits alone of the younger generation mark them off from their betters. What does an adult do when he feels like having a go at a detective story or the evening paper? Why, he picks out a convenient chair or props himself up on his pillows, arranges the light correctly for good vision, turns down the radio, and reaches for a cigarette or a piece of chocolate fudge.

Children, however, when the literary urge seizes them, take their comic books to the darkest corner of the room or else put their heads under the bedcovers. Nor do they sit *down* to read. They wander. They lie on the floor with their legs draped over the coffee table, or, alternatively, they sit on the coffee table and put the book on the floor. Or else they lean against the refrigerator, usually with the refrigerator door wide open. Sometimes I have seen them retire to closets.

Children in comfortable positions are uncomfortable—just as they are miserable if they can't also have the phonograph, the radio, the television and sometimes the telephone awake and lively while they pore on *The Monster of Kalliwan* or *The Jungle Book.*

But then, children don't walk like people, either—sensibly, staidly, in a definite direction. I am not sure they ever acquire our grown-up gaits. They canter, they bounce, they slither, slide, crawl, leap into the air, saunter, stand on their heads, swing from branch to branch, limp like cripples, or trot like ostriches. But I seldom recall seeing a child just plain walk. They can, however, dawdle. The longest period of recorded time is that interval between telling children to undress for bed and the ultimate moment when they have brushed their teeth, said their prayers, eaten a piece of bread and catsup, brushed their teeth all over again, asked four times for another glass of milk, checked the safety of their water pistols or their tropical fish, remembered there was something vital they had to confide to you, which they have forgotten by the time you reach their side, switched from a panda to a giraffe and back to the panda for the night's sleeping companion, begged to have the light left on in the hall, and finally, being satisfied that your screaming voice is in working order, fallen angelically into slumber.

Apprentice parents are warned to disregard at least nine-tenths of all such requests as pure subterfuge but to remember that maybe one of the ten is right and reasonable, like the night-light or the value of a panda when one is in a panda mood.

Not that reason weighs much with children. It is the great mistake we make with a child, to think progeny operate by our logic. The reasoning of children, although it is often subtle, differs from an adult's. At base there is usually a core of sanity, but one must disentangle what the lispers mean from what they say.

"I believe in Santa Claus," a daughter told me years ago, when she was five or six. "And I believe in the Easter Rabbit, too. But I just can't believe in Shirley Temple."

Until I worked out a solution for this enigmatic statement, I feared for the girl's mind. Then I realized that she had been watching the twenty-one-inch screen. After all, if you are six years old and see a grown-up Shirley Temple acting as mistress of ceremonies for a TV special one evening and the next day observe her, dimpled and brief-skirted, in an old movie, you are apt to find the transformation hard to credit.

I managed to unravel that utterance, but I never did pierce through to the heart of a gnomic pronouncement made by a young friend of hers. He meandered into the backyard one summer day when the whole family was preparing for a funeral. Our garden is thickly clustered with memorials to defunct wildlife, and on this particular afternoon we were intent on burying another robin.

John looked at the hole.

"What are you doing?" he asked, as if it weren't perfectly apparent to the most uninformed.

"Why, John," said my husband, "I'm digging a grave."

John considered the matter a while. Then he inquired again, with all the solemnity of David Susskind querying a senator, "Why don't you make it a double-decker?"

Not even Echo answered that one, but I kept my sense of proportion and went on with the ceremonies. You need a sense of proportion when dealing with children, as you also need a sense of humor. Yet you must never expect the very young to have a sense of humor of their own. Children are acutely risible, stirred to laughter by dozens of human mishaps, preferably fatal. They can understand the points of jokes, too, so long as the joke is not on them. Their egos are too new, they have not existed long enough in the world to have learned to laugh at themselves. What they love most in the way of humor are riddles, elementary puns, nonsense, and catastrophe. An elderly fat lady slipping on the ice in real life or a man in a movie falling from a fifteen-foot ladder equally transports them. They laugh at fistfights, clowns, people kissing each other, and buildings blowing up. They don't, however, enjoy seeing their parents in difficulties. Parents, they feel, were put on earth solely for their protection, and they cannot bear to have the fortress endangered.

Their peace of mind, their safety, rests on grown-up authority; and it is that childish reliance which invalidates the worth of reasoning too much with them. The longer I lived in a house with children, the less importance I put on cooperatively threshing out matters of conduct or explaining to them our theories of discipline. If I had it to do over again I wouldn't reason with them at all until they arrived at an *age* of reason—approximately twenty-one. I would give them rules to follow. I would try to be just, and I would try even harder to be strict. I would do no arguing. Children, in their hearts, like laws. Authority implies an ordered world, which is what they—and, in the long run, most of the human race—yearn to inhabit. In law there is freedom. Be too permissive and they feel lost and alone. Children are forced to live very rapidly in order to live at all. They are given only a few years in which to learn hundreds of thousands of things about life and the planet and themselves. They haven't time to spend analyzing the logic behind every command or taboo, and they resent being pulled away by it from their proper business of discovery.

When our younger and more conversational daughter turned twelve, we found she was monopolizing the family telephone. She would reach home after school at 3:14 and at 3:15 the instrument would begin to shrill, its peal endless till bedtime. For once we had the good sense neither to scold nor to expostulate. We merely told her she could make and receive calls only between five and six o'clock in the afternoon. For the rest of the day, the telephone was ours. We expected tears. We were braced for hysterics. What we got was a calm acceptance of a Rule. Indeed, we found out later, she boasted about the prohibition—it made her feel both sheltered and popular.

But, then, children are seldom resentful, which is another difference between them and people. They hold grudges no better than a lapdog. They are too inexperienced to expect favors from the world. What happens to them happens to them, like an illness; and if it is not too extravagantly unfair, they forget about it. Parents learn that a child's angry glare or floods of tears after a punishment or a scolding may send the grown-up away feeling like a despotic brute; but that half an hour later, with adult feelings still in tatters, the child is likely as not to come flying into the room, fling both carefree arms about the beastly grown-up's neck, and shout, "I love you," into her ear.

The ability to forget a sorrow is childhood's most enchanting feature. It can also be exasperating to the pitch of frenzy. Little girls return from school with their hearts broken in two by a friend's treachery or a teacher's injustice. They sob through the afternoon, refuse dinner, and go to sleep on tear-soaked pillows. Novice mothers do not sleep at all, only lie awake with the shared burden for a nightlong companion. Experienced ones know better. They realize that if you come down in the morning to renew your solacing, you will meet—what? Refreshed, wholehearted offspring who can't under*stand* what you're talking about. Beware of making childhood's griefs your own. They are no more lasting than soap bubbles.

I find myself hoaxed to this day by the recuperative powers of the young, even when they top me by an inch and know all about modern art. More than once I have been called long distance from a college in New England to hear news of impending disaster.

"It's exam time and I'm down with this horrible cold," croaks the sufferer, coughing dramatically. "Can you rush me that prescription of Dr. Murphy's? I don't trust our infirmary."

Envisioning flu, pneumonia, wasting fever, and a lily maid dead before her time, I harry the doctor into scribbling his famous remedy and send it by wire. Then after worrying myself into dyspepsia, I call two days later to find out the worst. An unfogged voice answers me blithely.

"What cold?" it inquires.

Ephemeral tragedies, crises that evaporate overnight are almost certain to coincide with adolescence. Gird yourselves for them. Adolescence is a disease more virulent than measles and difficult to outgrow as an allergy. At its onset parents are bewildered like the victim. They can only stand by with patience, flexibility, and plenty of food in the larder. It's amazing how consoling is a batch of cookies in an emergency. If it doesn't comfort the child, at least it helps the baker. I stopped in at a neighbor's house the other day and found her busily putting the frosting on a coconut cake.

"It's for Steven," she told me. "His pet skunk just died, and I didn't know what else to do for him."

Food helps more than understanding. Adolescence doesn't

really want to be understood. It prefers to live privately in some stone tower of its own building, lonely and unassailable. To understand is to violate. This is the age—at least for girls—of hidden diaries, locked drawers, unshared secrets. It's a trying time for all concerned. The only solace is that they do outgrow it. But the flaw there is that eventually they outgrow being children too, becoming expatriates of their own tribe.

For, impossible as it seems when one first contemplates diapers and croup, then tantrums, homework, scouting, dancing class, and finally the terrible dilemmas of the teens, childhood does come inexorably to an end. Children turn into people. They speak rationally if aloofly, lecture you on manners, condescend to teach you about eclectic criticism, and incline to get married. And there you are, left with all that learning you have so painfully accumulated in twenty-odd years and with no more progeny on whom to lavish it.

Small wonder we love our grandchildren. The old sage recognized the effect but not the cause. Enemies of our enemies indeed! They are our immortality. It is they who will inherit our wisdom, our experience, our ingenuity.

Except, of course, that the grandchildren's parents will listen benevolently (are they not courteous adults?) and not profit by a word we tell them. They must learn for themselves how to speak in another language and with an alien race.

17 • *The Sentimental Trap*

The hairdresser's salon is my lending library. Isled there in temporary peace underneath a gusty dryer, where no pot boils over and no telephone intrudes, I catch up with the week's crop of fashion magazines. It was in the glossiest of them not long ago I read an alarming paragraph. At least it alarmed me.

"Families," it chirruped, "should own traditions as well as roots. Ceremony is the cement of domestic life. Ritual treats—champagne at breakfast, say, on wedding anniversaries; daybreak serenades for Grandmother each May Day; winter Thermos-bottle picnics for the whole family, with sleds and snowball fights; an old-fashioned Fourth of July flag-raising—small things, every one. But they form the warm core of satisfying home relationships. Why not invent some such pretty custom?"

I pushed out of my mind the stimulating thought of snow down my neck with my lunch or of unwelcome pilgrimages to Grandmother's morning doorstep (*our* favorite ancestress sleeps till noon) and gave the author prompt answer right there where I was pampering my vegetable rinse.

"Because it's dangerous," I muttered. "Give tradition an inch and it takes your house."

As victim as well as lover of tradition, I know its perils.

Cement of domestic life it may well be. Yet pause a moment and remember that cement's most conspicuous quality is its tenacity. Invent a family custom, and you will no more be able to let it go than you can pull yourself out of quicksand. Children are the great conservatives. They want to keep everything forever—their oldest and most disgraceful toys, their dog-eared storybooks, the diaries they kept at nine, and always every feast they remember from infancy. Abandon one and they themselves feel abandoned. It has something to do with their unwillingness to grow older. Oh, they want to grow up, all right. They long to own the privileges of adulthood. But instinct warns them that once they quit the safe walls of childhood, all sorts of dragons, ogres, evil witches lurk in wait for them outside. So they cling to customs as young birds grip their nest in fear of flight.

Wise parents, therefore, will be slow to invent more annual festivities than they can handle later on. Bake one Epiphany cake, with its bean and its thimble and its coin for the lucky, and every Twelfth Night there must be another baking. Give one bob-for-apples party on Halloween and you'll be having to supply apples (and dry towels) each October 31 for the next decade. Light a Christmas tree in the patio when the oldest child is five and when she's married and a mother she'll still be expecting it.

No one knows this better than my husband and I. As a family we were for years martyrs to tradition. For us the turning year was a huge calendar splashed with red letters. We kept all holidays with as much pomp as a Mexican keeps his fiesta, and we were forever so busy hanging banners or lighting candles or roasting Thanksgiving turkeys and

Christmas geese that we had no energy left over to enjoy being spectators of our own jollity.

It all started, innocently enough, with a birthday. The birthday was mine; our marriage was a few months old, and my husband, still trailing clouds of glorious bachelorhood, went golfing. He not only went golfing but stayed on at the club to gloat over a low score. In the middle of genial reminiscence with his foursome (married men themselves, of an earlier vintage), he mentioned that really he ought to run along; there was an anniversary girl at home.

There fell a deep and startled silence.

Then, "My dear *boy*," they told him out of rich knowledge, "you really *should* run along."

My own behavior, I recall, was exemplary. I was composed, understanding, and speaking to him within a week. Still, the experience made a deep impression on us both. We agreed that an ideal household ought to be much as Yeats described it, a "place where all's accustomed, ceremonious." To me the idea was not new. I had been reared among my mother's people, a tradition-worshiping clan originally from southern Germany; I had cut my teeth on ceremony. He, however, youngest of nine in a family whose roots were half unsentimental Celtic, half taciturn New England, had thought holidays were merely occasions for catching up on one's sleep. But by nature he is an enthusiast. Once he discovered the mystique of feast-keeping, he embraced it with the zeal of a religious convert. Indeed, he embroidered it. We began to remember Days. There were Friday-night presents because we had been married on a Friday. We exchanged Valentines. Christmas trees shimmered in their proper season and we planted shrubs on Arbor Day. We raised flags for weekend guests. Thanksgiving was the time for inviting in unmarried friends to overeat. And that was all very well while there were two of us. We could acquire a custom and drop it again if it incommoded us. But presently there were three of us and then four and the case altered. The beguiling celebrations we invented so lightheartedly turned into, if not quite cement, at least a kind of glue—in which we stuck fast, like flies in syrup.

Take the matter of birthdays. It had been tempting to dazzle babies with cakes and tiny tapers and other babies to amuse them at their first three or four anniversaries. "After all," we told each other, "it is only birthdays which are singular to each individual. Let the child be the empress." So we stood her picture on the mantel with streamers extending from it to all four quarters of the living room. Further, crepe-paper festoons over doorways spelled out "Happy Birthday" to all comers. Her chair was decorated with bows and ribbons, and from that improvised throne she gave her queenly orders. For twelve delirious hours her word was law, particularly in the matter of menus. And that was splendid when her choice of a Lucullan banquet wavered between chopped beef with spinach and lamb chops accompanied by strained peas. It was when she asked for *crêpes Chantilly* in lieu of a cake that we felt the pinch.

By the same token, a collection of gifts was no problem when dolls or new coloring books were peaks of worldly desire. We also managed the necessary party with little more effort than it takes to launch a guided missile. Anybody in good health can bear up for an afternoon under the strain of entertaining a dozen overexcited tots if she girds herself for it and takes vitamins regularly. I just served food not too tempting to toss across the table, showed movies so quickly following the collation that the lights went off immediately after the cake-cutting, and eliminated boys. (Mixed parties were too much even for my holiday heart.) I also arranged that every guest got a prize, if for nothing more than owning the reddest hair or pinning the donkey's tail widest of the target. I urge these precautions on all tyro mothers of birthday children. Nothing can so puncture the party's joy as the wails of empty-handed six-year-olds competing unsuccessfully for a box of crayons or a twenty-five-cent soap-bubble pipe.

The trap began to close when birthday girls, growing up but still expecting royal privileges (which we had taught them), began mentioning solid-gold charm bracelets as appropriate gifts or suggesting a skiing trip to Vermont as a suitable party outing.

Revolt, however, had been stirring in my soul for some time. I looked about me and observed how festive clutter burdened the house. Closets bulged with holiday platters and tablecloths. Our attics overflowed with flags, streamers, horns of plenty, May baskets, Halloween costumes. The garden was awash with monuments to dead pets whom we buried with full processions and sermons. And it was always I who had to lug out, hang up, stow away each ritual implement. That's the thing you have to learn about children, the way you learn that the dog or the cat they could not live without and promised solemnly to care for sometimes goes hungry unless you set food in its tray. Children may give up believing in Santa Claus but never in the omnipotence of parents. That there is labor involved in helping them keep up treats and traditions does not occur to them until they are parents themselves.

My own birthday, for instance, they liked to imagine as

delightful as theirs. But who had to bake the cake, unearth the streamers, set the flowery table, tidy up the tissue-paper wrappings, and return to the stores the hosiery and bed jackets designed for a more Junoesque woman? If you need to ask, you are either no mother or else a great executive. I once hinted in a moment of madness that giving me breakfast in bed would be a welcome compliment on my Day. After one trial, I scotched that burgeoning custom before it could put out tentacles. What with wild cries from the kitchen of, "Where do we keep the *ba*-con?" and sounds below me of clashing cutlery or overturned egg cartons, with my tidbits arriving congealed and horrible on a newly chipped Meissen plate somewhere near lunchtime, I decided this was one celebrant who would rather come down for her gala.

Mother's Day was the same. I always rose with the lark that morning. Not only did I have to get into condition to accept the limp posies I knew would be plucked for me by grubby little hands, I had also to be prepared to open sentimental cards with grateful cries, cook a more elaborate dinner than usual, and get the chores out of the way early so that for the afternoon I could pass myself off under the disguise of Mother Resting.

So it went for the rest of the year's festivities—for St. Patrick's Day (real shamrocks in pots and a green table); Fourth of July, with its picnic; Decoration Day and parades; the Midsummer Eve's pagan bonfire; coming-out parties for childish molars. My husband gave immoderate help, but I was the housewife, and on me depended those redundant rites for burying broken mirrors with incantations and charms against bad luck, for feeding Thanksgiving guests, observing April Fools' Day, Bastille Day, Labor Day, Valentine's Day, February 22, and the anniversary of the Day We Adopted Our Poodle. I think the girls believed for a long time that Groundhog Day was a national holiday.

Even Easter's divine significance was blurred by the necessity for stuffed animals and egg hunts. I was rather bright, though, about the latter. Children are collectors, preferring quantity to quality, and since their object is to amass, the caprice can be expensive. I used a trick. We hid the eggs indoors, and I kept the baskets handy in my lap while the babies peered behind mirrors, under sofas, and back of pantry doors. As each little huntress fetched me her trophies, I quickly hid them again elsewhere. Given a bit of luck, I used to be able to keep the girls searching until time for their naps.

Still, such exercises were manageable. What brought on the shaking hands, the double vision was trying to live up to our family version of Christmas.

Slaves to tradition? We were bound to its tinsel wheel. Some lesser rituals had begun to drop away as the daughters went off to boarding school and college. My husband and I were able to be iconoclastic about our own anniversaries. But Christmas meant Coming Home, and to a home where existed an immutable program. There must be *springerle* and *lebkuchen* baked in our own kitchen in immemorial molds. The crèche must sit in its ordained site beside the fireplace, with the Wise Men progressing day by day toward Bethlehem. We must sing the same old carols on Christmas Eve, decorate identical lintels, shrubbery, the table, the chandeliers. Each member of the family must take possession of the same chair or sofa, sanctified over the years by personal use, for display of wrapped and mysterious gifts. Neither girl would give up the stuffed stocking which had to be filled by Mamma after we got back from midnight mass. And on the morning itself, ritual must never vary. My husband had to come down first to play "Oh, Come Little Children" on the piano, shout "Merry Christmas" from the foot of the stairs, pull the shades, and light three trees.

For did saner people struggle with one? We had them in matched sets, like guest towels—one for the living room which reached the ceiling; a small one in a stand which whirled like a carousel and played "Stille Nacht"; and one my husband had incautiously invented. It was made of heavy wire, draped with lighter strands. Some of the wires he had bent into loops which held in their cups fifty colored devotional candles. The skeleton we hung with out shiniest, prettiest baubles, so that the whole confection both made a conversation piece and gave a lovely light. But those fripperies took the better part of a week to put up and take down again. In addition, we had our silver horn to polish (it did not play but made a distinguished adornment for the front door), the mistletoe to hang in the hall, presents to provide for pets, tradesmen, and the postman. As a final task, there was always our Christmas china, which couldn't go into the dishwasher and had to be laundered by hand. My hand.

I suppose our original purpose in all this was not only to please the children but to make our house appealing to company. The trouble was that we spent so much time on decoration that we had none left for inviting in admiring guests. Christmas Day used to be rather vague to me. I walked through it in a haze of tiredness, barely able to take in its profane pleasures, let alone its greater meaning. It's possible *all* of us were tiring of ritual, but nobody would admit it. The only real sign of change was in getting-up habits. Once it was Father and Mother who were routed unwilling out at break of day by pretty squeals from the nursery. When daughters, though, have been out dancing four nights in a row, you can't expect them down to look at their loot much before noon.

I was brought to my senses by a revelation.

It happened one December morning, a week or two before the Noel.

When I woke it was snowing. Over the brown landscape great flakes fell like manna, translating winter's bleak geometry into a kind of abstract art. And even before I tasted the coffee which alone braces me to confront the naked day, I cried, relievedly, "Oh, wonderful! Maybe we'll have a white Christmas."

Forgotten were the inconveniences of a storm in the suburbs—chains, shovels, commuting trains off schedule, and grocery orders delayed. I remembered only that two college daughters would be home soon for the holidays. And while they would be too polite to reproach me, in each mind somehow the thought must lodge that if Mommy would just *try* a little harder, she could arrange snow for the twenty-fifth.

A second later I began to laugh outright. It was too ridiculous. Snow did not depend on me and neither did Christmas. When my reason had degenerated to the extent of planning to operate the weather, I was an addict—an addict of custom. It was time I kicked the habit.

That was the season I hid the monogrammed stockings and refused to hang a trinket. The girls, stunned and incredulous, but determined, between them set up the big tree in the living room, found the figures for the crèche and made halfhearted efforts at getting out the musical stand. But once Mother had revolted, with Father abetting her, ceremony did not seem half so essential to them. The next year we had one tree and last Christmas we forgot the mistletoe. We continue to polish the horn. The Wise Men still are moved forward each day toward the Stable, and we buy the cat her catnip mouse. We still sing a few carols and attend midnight services. But moderation has taken over. This year I even plan to invite the neighbors in for a party, so flowing am I with health and good will.

Still, habits leave their traces. I realized that we were all convalescent, not cured, when I heard a daughter talking not long ago to her husband, a recent family addition.

"Richard," she was saying dreamily, "what's your first real memory?"

I didn't catch his reply, but it must have suited her, for she went on with warmth in her voice. "Well, mine is coming into the living room on Christmas morning when I was about three and hearing music and seeing those lighted trees."

And then she added passionately, "Oh, let's do have special treats for *our* children. You know, birthday parties and family songs and Halloween masks and things. My sister and I had this crazy, wonderful childhood. We got tired of being indulged before the parents did, but it's something awfully happy to remember. Promise me we'll be that way, too."

Comforted, I turned away from my eavesdropping. Addicts we might have been. But perhaps the mania had been wholesome after all.

18 • Realms of Gilt

The children's library in our village is a charming spot. The room itself is spacious and sunny, its walls painted the color of spring apples, its chairs and tables and card catalogs all scaled to child size. The pair of patient librarians in charge are as ready to advise young minds as they are willing to hunt for mislaid mittens, replace lost cards, or zipper up snowsuits. On tiered shelves stand hundreds and hundreds of books—those books which flow out ceaselessly, year after year, from America's most respected presses. This, one would think, is Eden for a bookish child. But it is a flawed paradise. In all this treasury of the printed word, all this lavishness of binding and type and illustration, one lack diminishes the bounty. Much here is less than literature.

Children, of all people, deserve the best. At this age their tastes are forming. From the first nursery rhyme to the last Arthurian legend, they should have what even their elders do not often get in a story—accomplished style, honest motivation, characters proficiently drawn. And while those qualities can be found here if one searches, the mass of the writing is limp, listless, unoriginal, mediocre, and humdrum. Plots are insipid or mechanical. Too many pictures smother the story. And even when the writing lifts itself above accepted "juvenile" standards, its vigor is drained away by that leech among publishing structures—the Law of the Right Vocabulary.

I know; I am frequently a reader there. This was a province I investigated when my children were younger. I use it still, sometimes for research, sometimes for sociability, oftener for pure pleasure. For I am a great relisher of juveniles. The masterpieces among them never pall. They are the true escape literature, and in them one can run away to a genuine but different world, where virtue triumphs and struggle reaps its rewards. After all, there is only one test for a good book for children: can it be read without pain by an adult?

So now and then I compose myself (when some nine-day wonder of a contemporary novel has unsettled me) with the balm of remembered fantasy. Juveniles have a tonic value, like vitamins, restoring the mind's fabric. After finishing *Lolita* I read *Kim. The Sword in the Stone* soothed me after a session with *From the Terrace.* To turn from the desperation of Camus to the equally stoic but less-desperate philosophy of the spider in *Charlotte's Web* was pleasant as a brisk walk in the open air.

But I do not mistake such books for what on a child's level they are not—discussions of man's fate in symbols. Vast as it is, I read *Huckleberry Finn* without Freudian perceptions and for quite opposite reasons from *Moby Dick.* (Although I still believe with a young friend of mine that the latter "is a very interesting treatise on whaling.") I enjoy *Alice's Adventures in Wonderland* because I enjoy nonsense. I like *The King of the Golden River* and *Mary Poppins* and *The Peterkin Papers* and *Sarah Crewe* and *The Prince and the Pauper* and *Jemima Puddleduck* and *The Princess and the Goblins* and *The Jungle Book*, and I like them for what they remain in their own right—entrancing fiction.

The pity is that more first-rate authors do not write for children. They have done so in other eras without apology. Dickens was generous to the young, and so were Thackeray and Browning and Mark Twain. Lang and Ruskin and Belloc and Lear never disdained to amuse their juniors. In our day the initialed Whites, both E. B. and T. H., have delighted them; not to speak of James Thurber, Mary Chase, Pearl Buck, Rumer Godden, Elizabeth Enright, C. S. Lewis, and Ludwig Bemelmans. But the majority of distinguished literary figures of the present seem not to have entertained a thought that children are the finest audience in the world. For that is what they are —enormous in numbers, avid for fulfillment, and immensely loyal. Children consider one perusal of a book only the aperitif before the meal. No wonder a cliché for a juvenile is "dog-eared." The well-loved book in a child's library is invariably that—worn, used, carried to bed, fetched to the table, even nostalgically borne off to college years after it was first purchased.

Children are also something better than loyal—they are adventurous. Something rich and strange delights them. One of my daughters was recovering, at five, from chicken pox when I first realized how little hazard one runs in letting children stretch the muscles of their minds. As a convalescent, she demanded the right to be read to. At hand was *The Wind in the Willows*, and I started in on the adventures of Mr. Toad. After a chapter or two, though, I began to have misgivings. The adventures were satisfactory, but Kenneth Grahame had not been tutored in the new school of talking down to children. His vocabulary, his wit, his plotting gave no quarter to limited comprehension.

"Look, dear," I said, preparing to shut the pages, "these are awfully hard words. I think the book is too old for you."

The patient was not only firm, she was distraught. "I don't care," she cried. "I don't *care* if it's too hard for me. I don't care if I can't understand the words. I just want to hear that story."

Yet the publishing business goes on believing the new Commandment: "Thou shalt not mystify."

A novelist friend of mine, who has written a pair of notable children's stories, tells me that while she was visiting her publishers she wandered through the juvenile department, looking over the shoulders of copy editors hard at work. One of them was busily referring to a manuscript and a syllabus, scratching out and rewriting like a schoolmistress with a term paper.

"Running into trouble?" my friend inquired casually. "Don't tell me there's a censorship problem in juveniles!"

"Oh, certainly," said the scribe. "We have to be *very* careful. Here is a book intended for children from six to nine. And this paper contains all the words that six-to-nine-year-olds are supposed to be able to understand. I have to take out all the big words not on the list and put in little ones."

My friend was so horrified that she made a vow then and there she would write no more for such a market.

It is the stranglehold of the "right vocabulary" which has probably done more than anything else to frighten worthwhile authors away from a field which could yield so rich a creative harvest.

Whose invention was this vocabulary restriction I cannot say. Librarians deplore the trend, publishers disclaim responsibility, authors declare themselves stifled by it, children detest it. But the fact remains that somebody has set up as gospel the rule that odd words, long words, interesting words, grown-up words must be as precisely sifted out from a book for, say, five-year-olds as chaff from wheat or profanity from a television program. The law, I am glad to say, is often joyfully and profitably broken. But the restraints stand. "Read-it-yourself" books now come cleverly planned around a vocabulary of three hundred fifty words or thereabouts, and the fact that they are often clever and occasionally brilliantly ingenious does not alter their crippling formula.

Are children never to climb? Must they be saved from all the healthy bumps and bruises of exploration? I suppose the theory drifted down from textbooks, those teacher's-college-tested readers which are the common and insipid fare of elementary schools. Like many bad things, they were inspired by good intentions. Children, said the educationalists, must be gently led along the path to learning, seduced not prodded. So a vocabulary must be acquired in standard stages and according to procedures formed in a laboratory and stamped out by IBM machines. Probably modern textbooks are placider than *Fox's Book of Martyrs* or the theological treatises on which little Pilgrims used to sharpen their wits. But they cater only to the average or below-average mind. The genuine reading child is not an average person, and he wants, even at six or seven or eight, gourmet fare. Yet so prophylactic has the whole business become that the good sap of invention is being squeezed out of both storybooks and schoolbooks. In cutting down the weeds we have also cut down the flowers.

And we have done more than smother word discovery; we have deleted magic and fantasy from children's lives. Most modern textbooks try to appeal to the young by talking about what they already know—their everyday activities.

"Bill Carter's Map" is the title of a story in one second-grade reader I picked up recently. And it begins:

> Bill Carter drew a map and took it to school. The map showed his teacher where Bill lives.
>
> First he drew Main Street. Then he drew Indian Road. Bill drew a small picture for his house. He drew a bigger picture for the school.
>
> Bill marked NORTH and SOUTH on his map. Is Bill's house south of the school?

This was not a civics textbook, you understand, but something supposed to lead young minds into the green fields of literature. I can only believe that a seven-year-old must be as bored by it as I was.

Compare such an opus with the beginning of a story from the ancient treasure called *Second Eclectic Reader* designed by that often-ridiculed genius, William H. McGuffey, well over a hundred years ago.

The story is called "Mr. Post and Mary," and it begins in good, sound, melodramatic-fiction fashion:

> One cold night, after old Mr. Post had gone to bed, he heard a noise at the door.

He went out to see what it was; and what do you think he found?

He found a little babe on the door step, crying with the cold.

Now which of the two texts do you think would keep the eyes of the embryo reader fastened to the page, trying to find out What Happened? The second, of course. McGuffey may seem outdated and unskilled in pedagogy to modern educators. But he taught several generations of frontiersmen to value literature, and he had the root of the matter in him. He knew that readers are not formed by monotony of material. Children don't really care to learn in second grade that Bill's house is south of the school. They want excitement, verve, action in their narratives, even if it is embodied by an orphan baby on a doorstep. If they do not find it in their school readers and their library fiction, they will turn to the eternal comics and perhaps remain only half-literate all their lives. They will be unable to spell out a message unless it is accompanied by a picture.

Which brings me to another unhappy thing which has happened to the juvenile literature of the era: books have become nonbooks; not volumes of reading material but mere objects. While the pop-up and the pullout and other such disturbing lunacies have rightly dwindled in popularity, the overillustrated book remains.

Randolph Caldecott, that great altruist, could scarcely have known what he was unleashing on the world when he revolutionized bookmaking for the young back in the early nineteenth century.

The children's books of that period had been like the children's clothes—small copies of adult styles. They were heavy to read and dull to look at. Caldecott (like Kate Greenaway a little later) was a reformer who quite properly decided that children should be catered to by eye and ear. He turned out gems of illustrative art. What he did not do, one trusts, is envision the future of his project.

For now the tail wags the dog. It is illustration rather than story which again and again determines a book's success. In matters of format, design, and color, the young are sumptuously regaled. Never has so much talent and expense gone into making picture books really books of pictures. But now it is the artist and not the writer who has become important out of all proportion. This would be splendid if the desired end of reading were the formation of a taste for good art. But these are books, meant to whet the child's appetite for literature. Unless a text measures up to its decoration, the young will not become real readers, ever.

I am certain that children, left to themselves, would prefer a rattling good story with black and white illustrations, or even none at all, to the handsomest volume in the world which brings no glory to their dreams or quickening to their pulses. I would suggest that publishers, if they wish to print the best, spend less money on six-color pictures and more on persuading writers of substance to invent good tales. I would have them look around for a new Kipling.

And I would tell those same publishers to forget entirely about which combination of letters is suitable for the mind of a child at a specified age. Children afraid of new words? Absurd! Readers-to-be love them. They may stumble on them now and then, but who cares about stumbling in the delightful race toward knowledge? They may mispronounce, but where's the harm in that?

I have a daughter who used to say "biss-hop" instead of "bishop" because that's the way the noun looked to her, and a very distinguished epithet we found it. A young acquaintance once complained that the heroine of her story had been "mizzled" which seemed infinitely more eloquent than "mis-led." Neither child grew up to be a Mrs. Malaprop.

Children are explorers by nature. They have to be in order to discover the world around them. What kind of an expedition is it and to what dreary climates must they plod if their fiction contains nothing new and strange and mysterious—not even new and strange and mysterious words?

If ever I had time and courage enough, I'd write a children's book stuck plum-pudding rich with great jawbreakers of words. I would use "egregious." I would work in "monstriferous." I would use "sepicolous" and "ubiquitous" and "antidisestablishmentarianism" and "nictate" and "supernumerary" and "internecine" and a hundred glorious others. And I think children would get the joke and flock to it—if, that is, the story were good enough. They are a braver generation than we suppose.

So they deserve brave books. They deserve the best that men and women of wit and talent can write for them. If the millennium ever arrives, it will be on the juvenile shelves that the new Homers and Dantes and Shakespeares will happily sit. There must be something we can all do to hurry the day along.

19 • *Manners Are Morals*

When you ask a question of life, it isn't often you get a straight and immediate answer. Last week, however, I made such a query and received a response as patly as if a stage director had arranged it. Both events happened on visits; and the first was rather an unsettling experience. I had dropped in for tea with a friend down the street, to find her in tears.

"It's Elaine and the children," she confided to me, wiping her eyes on a napkin. "They were all over here this morning, and we had a disagreement."

I knew my friend's daughter-in-law, a delightful young woman of impeccable breeding. I had also encountered her pair of flaxen-haired, rosy-cheeked young fiends in human form, so I picked my way with care among consolatory sentences.

"Being a grandmother is a mixed blessing," I said cautiously. "It's the difference in the generations. When Monica and Tony are old enough to have some manners, everything will be easier."

"That's the trouble," my friend wailed. "Elaine thinks teaching them manners is nonsense. She told me so when I was trying to persuade Monica to butter her bread like a lady instead of stuffing a whole slice into her mouth. Elaine says her life was nearly ruined by being brought up so rigidly—calls it the 'white-glove syndrome.' *He* children aren't going to live by all those silly rules, sh says. She claims it's self-reliance and character she's afte not frills."

I mumbled something noncommittal about inhibition and psychology and everything turning out right in th end. But my hostess was too agitated to be fobbed off wit such dubious comfort.

"I know she's wrong, but the stupid thing is I can' think of a good argument to contradict her. If manner are nothing but frills, Elaine is perfectly justified. I sup pose we *don't* have time for frills in this age. It's so awfu though," and here my friend relapsed into real despair. " just know those two are going to grow up horrid, oafis people—and I can't bear it!"

"Oh, well," I said awkwardly, "they'll probably tur out as charming as their mother—and their grandmothe —in spite of Elaine's theories. Children do, you know."

For at the moment, like her, I could think of nothin constructive with which to parry her daughter-in-law' raw logic. Kind hearts are obviously more than coronet and character of greater importance than the ability t handle a piece of bread and butter gracefully. There wa a fallacy somewhere, but I couldn't put a reasonable finge on it; that is, not a finger Elaine would be willing to follow

The answer was handed to me a day or two later on trip through the New England countryside. I had stoppe off to visit a boarding school for girls where the Headmis tress is a friend of mine and where some of my family hav been educated. This is an old school as American establish ments go, and its customs tend to linger. In spite of it formidably modern equipment—chalk-fragrant classroom precise laboratories, acres of hockey fields—tradition still wreathes it tighter than the woodbine on its brick walls. And the Head's domain changes no more than do the rules The wide hall smells the same as always of furniture polish, books, and children. The stairs still sweep grandly down from a mysterious upper floor of offices and dormitories. And it was on this formal stairway that I saw a girl go through an acrobatic performance as absurd as it was charming.

She was in uniform, of course, her arms burdened with books, on her way in a rush to some desperate student goal. Then she encountered the Head and me. And caught so in mid-flight, balanced improbably on one step, clumsy with her great load of papers and texts, she still managed what custom there demanded. She put one foot behind her and dropped a ritual curtsy. It took courage and it took athletic skill. It was also, I felt, quite ridiculous. I murmured something of the sort to the Head.

"You still have them doing it, I see. And do they still get demerits if they forget?"

She looked at me with amusement. "Yes, my dear, they do—and I know exactly what you're thinking A Victorian relic, quite useless so far as jobs and College Boards are concerned. We have it out in committee every year."

"Well," I confessed, "you have to admit it's pretty inessential. A curtsy in this day and age—*and* on the stairs. It's appealing but does it really count?"

"Good manners always count," said the Head serenely. "We could omit the curtsy, if you like. It's only a school ceremony. But we can't drop this drill on manners. It's one way of teaching morality."

"Morality?"

"Certainly." Her voice was gentle but assured. "Manners and morals are all of a piece. One is only proof of the other. That child you smiled at just now wasn't doing just a difficult gymnastic stunt. She was showing respect to superior wisdom, sagacity, and"—here the Head glanced at me slyly—"age."

"But she was in a hurry," I protested. "And it's such a—such a *salute*."

"Artificial, you mean? Quite true. But you don't object to saluting the flag, do you? She was doing honor to another sort of standard—our importance. And who knows? If we keep on training her, these manners, the curtsies and respectful answers and artificial niceties, may become something more than automatic reflexes. Her heart may be touched as well. She may learn really to respect authority and wisdom, value courtesy for its own sake, as well as go through the motions."

I thought it over for a moment. "You mean a gesture can instruct the mind?"

"We think so here," said the Head. "We believe in the philosophy that 'you become what you imitate.' Children learn the multiplication table by rote before they understand the theory of numbers. And we can also teach them certain physical responses before they are clever enough or good enough to understand genuine kindness. The young are hardhearted, you know. Selfishness has to be exercised out of them."

I laughed to myself as I was driving home, being particularly polite to other cars on the highway, as I always am after a session with the Head, whose exquisite manners are contagious. How revolted Elaine would have been with that exhibition! It was her loathed white-glove Syndrome at its most exaggerated. And yet, I mused, waving a too-eager driver past me at the intersection, were the two women so far apart in their aims? Both wanted their children to grow up to be people of worth. It was in their methods they so ludicrously differed. But where Elaine was reacting, the Head was acting. And it seemed to me that for all her unworldliness, reality stood naked at her side. She had, in fact, given me that answer Elaine's mother-in-law and I had tried unsuccessfully to phrase. I could scarcely wait to pour out to my friend this brand-new rebuttal for the theory that manners were unimportant.

Unimportant? They were vital. A quiet woman in a New England school had made it seem quite clear. For all that curtsies might be out of date, white gloves no longer necessary for a Sunday call, what Elaine had damned as frills—soft answers; inoffensive customs at table; courtesy to one's elders, betters, equals, and inferiors—were simple practical evidence of the kind hearts she valued and the solid character she desired to build. They were the first small steps to the house of merit in which she truly wanted them to live.

"Demonstrations of virtue," I said aloud. "That's what good manners ought to be. And nobody can learn them too young."

Tooling along the road at a legal fifty miles an hour, I began to sort those virtues out in my head. Chiefly I classified the ones which had bearing on my friend's problem, her grandchildren's upbringing.

Since for me morality had been conveniently packaged a long while ago in something called the Ten Commandments, I ran through the ancient list. Which would Elaine accept as valid? Not, probably, the one which mentions honoring thy father and thy mother and therefore all one's seniors. To her it would seem as outdated as the polka. Elaine, I reflected, was really a bit behind the times. She subscribed to a brand of thought, already discredited, which wished from children not honor but comradeship—and would likely receive neither. She would be amused but not shocked by an anecdote told me a decade ago by a friend who taught in a school where permissive behavior had its apotheosis.

One of the parents had called in at noon to speak to the principal. She was caught in the corridors by a surging crowd of hungry adolescents on their haring journey to the cafeteria, resistless as lemmings. She was jostled, pushed out of the way, finally knocked down completely. Her bag spilled open, her hat was trod on. And out of the mob only one boy rushed to her relief. He helped her get dazedly to her feet, brushed off her clothes, and handed her back her hand bag. Just as she was feeling herself gingerly for broken bones, an instructor hurried up, panting with confusion and chagrin.

"Oh, I *am* so sorry," she cried. "You must excuse that boy. He's new here."

Apocryphal or not, it remains a story which explains much about the manners of a generation just coming to maturity. It explains also why parents like me and *my* generation fought such lonely skirmishes along the behaviorist front. Flinching from automatic "I won't's" and "You can't make me's" of the young, we had to evolve our own alibis for wielding unfashionable authority. In our own family, we just decided that so long as we were bigger and stronger than our offspring, it behooved them to do as we said. An even firmer couple I know pointed out to their brood that the hand which held the purse strings wrote the rules. How much easier it would have been and still would be if good manners—a respectful tongue, an attentive ear, obedience this side of slavishness—were equated with morality. Then there would be no need to invent excuses for curbs and disciplines. However, understanding the Elaines of this world, I resignedly ruled out the oldest and most dignified of natural laws and went on to more specific ones.

Thou shalt not steal, I considered. Couldn't that be stretched to fit a lot of things? Being tidy in one's room, not using the phone too much, changing from school clothes to blue jeans for play, taking care of other people's property?

And recalling the time when Monica, at my house, had ingeniously detached a Meissen cup from its hook in the china cabinet and broken the handle, with no more than an unconcerned cluck from her mother as reprimand, I added, breaking and entering is a felony any way you look at it. You could point that out to children.

Quarrels, too—you might stop a lot of them if everybody was reminded that we aren't supposed to covet or be angry or bear false witness.

Good breeding does not raise its voice in controversy. It refrains from temper tantrums. It does not call its brother "fool." But it is the moral law which instigated the good breeding in the first place, not the other way round. The soft answer and the reasonable apology, the control of one's own ego—the social animal acquired those after he had acquired a belief in theological virtues. Savages have no manners. And children are savages until they have learned to imitate the civilized.

None of those things would be good enough to convince Elaine, I thought. If I just told her flatly that anger is a major sin, she would say sin is relative. Or else nonexistent.

Still, Elaine, however dogmatic about psychological shibboleths, was a notably splendid young woman with a social conscience. There was one enormous virtue she believed in with all her heart.

Charity, I thought with the clarity of revelation. She believes in charity, And that's what manners prove.

Thank heaven and democratic progress, charity is one traditional virtue the modern world is willing to applaud. But what a lot we talk about it these days, and how often we miss its implications. Charity is not simply a donation to the community chest and a gift to the Hundred Neediest Cases at Christmastime. It is not merely giving one's hours as a volunteer in a hospital or subscribing to the relief of flood victims a hemisphere away. It is both larger and smaller than those things, at once easier and harder, and it does, indeed, begin at home. Charity is graciousness and tact. Charity is a guarded tongue. It is picking up one's toys, giving a hand with the dinner dishes, writing a bread-and-butter letter to one's hostess. It is turning off television at a respectable hour so one's neighbor can sleep in peace, and being patient with bores. It is thanking salesladies in shops, forbearing to pass on the bit of malicious gossip so tempting to tell, wielding knife and fork so that we do not aesthetically offend.

"Charity suffereth long, and is kind; charity envieth not;

charity vaunteth not itself, is not puffed up," wrote St. Paul. He might well have added that charity (before it progresses to such great bounties and is still a child) first learns not to monopolize the telephone, comes when it is called, asks leave to go to the movies or to use the car, remembers that adults have nerves and frustrations too, and is agreeable to guests in the house.

At the school where the Head presides, Consideration for Others is noted on report cards along with Promptness, English Aptitude, and Mathematical Improvement. Once I had been beguiled by the quaintness of the phrasing. Now it seemed to me to embody the total of man's social duty, as well as childhood's great necessary training. It is the essence of charity as it is the essence of good manners. It is even the heart of law.

Since the truth seemed so obvious, why, I wondered as I turned into my own driveway, have we allowed ourselves so long to be beckoned off into different and absurd directions about behavior? For Elaine was not singular. She was only literal; and she was only literally construing the educational doctrines of the past twenty-five years. We wanted our young to stand on their own feet. We forgot about vulnerable toes they might tread on in the process. We wished they might be strong-minded, confident, resolute, capable of carrying burdens. We overlooked the fact that strength of mind is a discipline, resolution must learn sacrifice, and that the burden we most need to bear is our neighbor's good. To Elaine, "white gloves" referred to young men who jumped from their chairs when a woman stood, who said "sir" to their seniors, flourished a lighter for every cigarette, opened the doors of cars and restaurants for girls and women, did not assert their opinions too loudly in adult company, and put on neckties for dinner; but in whom prejudice thrived and conformism flourished. It meant young women who knew the right fork to use for a fish course but nothing about human rights, who had been to dancing school and who deferred prettily to their mothers' friends but could not carry on an intellectual conversation, who kept their gloves white and their opinions vaguely gray.

She was guilty of false reasoning, I decided, as I locked the garage doors and wandered, still bemused, up the stairs and into the kitchen, where presently I must assemble an evening meal. Urbane gestures do not by themselves make philosophers or saints, but they do not unmake them either. In fact, the saints were almost all of them celebrated for courtesy. Francis de Sales, for instance. So silken were his manners that they almost obscured the hard fact of his holiness. Loyola charmed friends and enemies alike; Assisi's Francis was polite even to the wolves of the forest and the mice in his cell. Because young people were trained to automatic pleasantries, it did not follow they would lose the sterner virtues. A courtly person is not by definition a shallow person, nor is a rude one better for his rudeness. Indeed, rudeness implies egotism, which is the exact opposite of charity. Opening car doors means nothing in itself. Letting an older woman precede one into a room means nothing. But preparing the mind for kindnesses by teaching such flourishes does mean a great deal. Character is a sturdy cloth woven of hundreds of threads, and every thread is important. Elaine was permitting Monica and

Tony to weaken that cloth by forcing them to make no effort at sacrifice or control.

"A gentleman is a person who never unwittingly offends" runs the old epigram from a more cynical age. If one is old-fashioned enough to use the word *gentleman* nowadays, he might better be defined as one who does not offend at all—not by crass manners at table or intrusions into other people's conversations or by discourtesy even to those who deserve it.

"Frills, frills, I could hear Elaine replying impatiently to my arguments. "What about world peace? What about social justice? What about race relations? How can learning to drop a curtsy or hold one's tongue help in those terribly urgent reforms?"

"Reformers get further when they do not antagonize," I might tell her. And it would be true. But I knew a simpler answer. I could point to an example in the school where the Head had dominion—one so easy and pleasant and subtle that I had forgotten it *was* an example.

Among all the teachers there, the children have a favorite. She takes the fourth class, trains the choir, and is so beloved that the girls yield to her an automatic duty they sometimes give grudgingly to lesser instructors. She is also a Negro, as beautiful and dark as a tribal queen. Surely children growing up there in that aura of good breeding, dropping her a curtsy in the classroom or on the stairs, giving her their hearts and their obedience, are learning as much about correct race relations as if they carried banners in parades or sat in at segregated lunch counters. They are doing better than that. They are forgetting such a thing as racial separation exists.

"Manners *are morals,*" I repeated aloud, as I took the lamb chops out of the refrigerator and made sure the lettuce was thoroughly dried for the salad. "They are the exercises of the body for the sake of the mind and soul."

It would be something sound to tell my friend. It would be something excellent to remember for myself. And while I was on the subject of manners, I would that minute set about trying to improve my own.

20 · *Keeping Up with the Joneses, Jr.*

Every now and then when I am in a benign mood, I stop to count my blessings. I give thanks for friends and for drip-dry underwear; for the sun in the morning and my new electric blanket at night; for my dentist, my husband, my automatic pencil sharpener. But chiefly I am grateful that I don't have to be a child in this era.

Youth is a perfectly wonderful commodity and far too valuable, as Shaw has pointed out, to be wasted on the young. Yet like all human benefactions, it has its penalties, which in today's urgent society have frighteningly increased. I don't think I am merely nostalgic when I contend that being a child nowadays is a tougher proposition than it was when my generation and I compared arithmetic answers between classes or devoured bread-and-pickle sandwiches on the front porch after school. For one thing, it isn't as much fun.

On the surface this assertion may sound like gibbering nonsense. Never before in history has childhood had so much attention paid to its welfare and its amusement. It is cosseted, pampered, immunized against unhappiness as against polio or whooping cough.

Also on the surface, its pattern of traditional play seems

not to have changed very much since my time—or since Tom Sawyer's or Alexander's. Little boys still scuffle on pavements with friends as truculently as if they were enemies. Little girls, curls or pigtails bobbing, still swing ropes to identical chants I remember, leaping like dervishes at the climactic command of "Salt, Vinegar, Mustard—PEPPER!" Baseballs thud into gloves too large for hands they encase. Kites fly, forts get built out of snow, summer waters divide where frolicking bodies flash through them like dolphins. But there is a difference in the way the games are played.

That nimble child with the skip rope may not be bounding merely for the pleasure of physical activity. Perhaps she practices leaps so that at ballet class on Saturday morning she can improve her *tour jeté* and be able to star in the spring show. There is a contest arranged for kite flyers, with cash awards donated for the winners by the chamber of commerce—so reeling a paper toy in and out of the sky is serious business. The champion builder of snowmen has his picture in the paper. That ballplayer exercises his arm apprehensively. Will he or will he not be included in a Little League, where he and the rest of his team can own uniforms and a coach and listen to parents cheering from genuine grandstands? The swimmer vies for medals. Those vague dreams and rewards of "When I grow up" have suddenly become concrete goals, scaled to child's size. The play has turned professional. And the ordinary competitive instinct of the young is being channeled into a frenzy of keeping up with, or learning to surpass, all the little Joneses in the neighborhood.

There is nothing wrong with healthy competition. But

there is, it seems to me, something both wrong and unwholesome about harassing those below their teens into too early insistence on success. A success, that is, imposed from above. In the same society which has made so much recent outcry about the perils of conformity in the adult world, a kind of terrible conformity of effort is being forced upon youth.

Not all boys are natural material for Little League, and thank God for it. Not all little girls are born to be prima ballerinas. Olympic standards in swimming or hurling a ball or brandishing a tennis racket are not for everyone. Left to themselves, the duffers might find some field in which they could excel—making up stories for younger brothers and sisters, maybe, or naming wild flowers, or just rejoicing in their own thoughts. But they are *not* left to themselves. No quarter is given to the dilettante.

A bookish nine-year-old girl I know was discovered lying face down on her bed one spring afternoon not long ago, alternately crying her heart out and exclaiming, as if she were the heroine of a Victorian novel, "In vain! In vain! All in vain!"

Her matter-of-fact mother told me about it with amusement, but I was appalled by the reason for the tears. The child's heart had been broken, not for any realistic tragedy (like being left out of a party list or receiving few Valentines in the school Valentine box). She had simply, after hours of practice, trailed the field in the fourth-grade square-dancing competition. She had chasséd left when she was supposed to promenade right or made some such other public faux pas. The shame was more than she could bear.

Had so much stress not been laid on conforming to a

pattern, she wouldn't have cared a fig about her *dos-à-dos*. It wasn't her talent, and she ought not to have minded. I can recall, for instance, being the worst map drawer for my age and weight in the whole school when I was a fourth grader. I was also the clumsiest volleyball player on our side when we chose up teams at recess. But no iron entered my soul. If my maps were lopsided, at least I got A's on my compositions. And if I couldn't knock the ball back across the net two-thirds of the time, I was valued by my contemporaries in spite of it because I made up such involved signals for Saturday games of Run, Sheep, Run. No parent, no teacher, was breathing down my neck, expecting me to beat a community record in some field. The most irksome admonition I received was an exasperated, "Do take your nose out of that book and get into the fresh air." And while such tolerance kept me from perfecting my swimming stroke, made me the eternal amateur at sports, it left my self-confidence intact. I went on, however ineptly, building my snow forts and turning my ankles skating on winter ice and floundering in warm ponds as happily as if I were champion of every art. I was following Chesterton's sound advice that "whatever is worth doing is worth doing badly."

That is what today's generation is not permitted. Fear of failure is indoctrinated in them early—nor is it only fear of failure at games. Socially, also, children are expected to star, are required to follow a pattern exact as a diet list. Are bananas good for twelve-week-old babies? Is strained liver prescribed a little later, whole milk at eight months? Well and good. There is a chart for gregarious behavior just as rigid. At seven, little girls ought to start casting warm looks on their favorite cub scout. At nine, they should be inviting "mixed groups" to their birthday galas. They must master the day's approximation of the waltz or the Twist at, say, eleven, and no later than twelve months afterwards wangle from some masculine contemporary in junior high school an invitation to the movies. At thirteen or fourteen, they should have turned into accomplished sirens.

If the pattern does not become them, if they are more interested in books or tropical fish than in experimenting with lipstick, mothers wring hands over their predilection for spinsterhood. When I was a tomboy in middy blouse and pleated skirt, no such precocious behavior was demanded of us. Boys might carry home our book bags or help us with geography lessons; they might even be invited in for a casual piece of chocolate cake by hospitable mothers. But little girls too given to giggles and melting glances were earmarked "boy-struck" and their conduct frowned on. Today, though, if there is a Thelma Jones in the neighborhood who has known from her cradle how to toss an alluring tress over her shoulder and assure the class hero that he is Tarzan and Hector and Socrates all rolled into one, she is called "socially adjusted." And it is Thelma whom her peers are urged to emulate. Even the boys, sturdy bachelors of ten or eleven, are prodded into following paths their elders think suitable. To be a boy scout now, it is not enough to stay reverent, courteous, and clean; to camp ecstatically if uncomfortably in sleeping bags; and to track the fierce woodchuck down spring trails. A loyal scout must also attend the troop's two dances a year, complete with date.

(Their opposite numbers, with true feminine excess, have gone farther. The Girl Scouts of America have just announced the formation of a new group, the Cadettes, who will study not marching and good deeds, but how to get along with young men and the most efficient ways of applying cosmetics.)

That children might want to wait a while before they cast off childhood is scarcely taken into consideration by schools, parents, community leaders, busy keeping little Joneses on their mettle. It is now possible to be a social failure earlier than twelve. Girls learn to be wallflowers before their petals open and boys to retreat into premature misogyny with voices still unbroken.

They can also be academic failures as early as kindergarten. For prosperous middle-class America has suddenly discovered the prestige of education and is bowing down before it as before a golden calf. I am not, naturally, against education. To enlarge and elevate the mind, particularly the child mind, is the noblest of all human activities. Moreover, the hungry intelligence of youth has always been able to assimilate more learning than our schools were prepared to feed it. What I deplore is the new race toward measured achievement, the frantic struggle of all parents to set their children competing for grades, marks, triumphs in aptitude tests, not for the love of knowledge, but because only triumph will get them into future colleges.

That the struggle has innocent motives, that the snobbery of a high IQ proceeds from a good cause does not reduce tensions for the children involved. There used to be room in childhood's world for every kind of mentality. If schools offered less challenge in my day than in this, at least they gave to us, who sat in unassorted classrooms, a kind of anonymous safety. We were not branded by the Test. Now the specter of the intelligence test, the examination for aptitude, achievement, special skills, hangs over our schools like a nightmare, haunting our young from the time they enter first grade until they walk onstage for a diploma. Tests sort them, classify them, winnow them out as if they were gradable peas from a commercial garden. Into one compartment go the jumbo-sized IQ's; into another the medium, into a third the inferior. And the fact that such tests measure neither leadership nor talent nor emotional adjustment, nor even promise, stops no educator from doing the classifying—nor the sortee from feeling its impact. Again, success or failure comes too soon.

"Jane isn't a student," Jane's mother used to say with a lenient smile. She knew perfectly well Jane could straggle on somehow toward graduation, no doubt marry young, and let fall her lines in pleasant places. Jane was able to wear her academic inability gaily, as if it were a corsage.

Or, "Howard's impossible at math," Howard's father was inclined to boast. "Just like his old man. But you ought to see the way he'll hit that scrimmage line when he gets to Princeton."

Now Howard, Sr., is having his eight-year-old son tutored in arithmetic, burdening him with summer-school lessons, making him feel guilty of some juvenile sin for not achieving the same marks as the Jones lad. He is aware, and makes the boy aware, that there will be no Princeton in his future—perhaps not even a Siwash University—unless things improve. Jane's mother, eager for the prestige a good college bestows now on a girl (socially, important as a debut), is nagging her daughter into hysterics or moving her from school to school, hoping somehow to redesign her charming if unscholarly mind. No wonder the neuroses of childhood increase and unsuccessful victims of the System turn delinquent at twelve. One needs an adult shell to withstand the knowledge that the path one walks will lead into no enchanted land. And even for the successful, some of the fun of undetermined aims has vanished.

I know a young woman with four children all still under six. She lives in a delightful suburb but is deserting it for Larkspur Manor. In Larkspur Manor she has no friends, her house will not be so attractive as the one she owns.

"But Larkspur has this awfully good school," she admits candidly. "The principal gets practically the entire senior class into college. I have to think ahead."

Already, you see, she is waging that battle for status. Higher education is not a dim vision on a faraway horizon but a prize for which the battle begins in the perambulator. And the prize is a pragmatic one—a social rather than an intellectual reward. Her brood will be trained for winning scholastic merit as they will be groomed for appearance and poise. First-rate schooling has to her the identical value of orthodontics, summer camps, riding lessons, and a talking doll for the baby. It is a Thing which she competitively tries to buy for them, like a rocking horse.

She is not unique. The operative word in juvenile upbringing today is Things. American children are afflicted with a glut of possessions. Peer into any ordinary middle-class nursery. Its material accumulations overwhelm the grown-up who remembers from her own youth how exciting it was to receive, say, a new set of paper dolls, or how the neighborhood Midas swaggered when he finally came into his inheritance of a real catcher's mask and glove.

My childhood was not deprived, except by current standards. But it was certainly not animated by all the fire engines, dolls, educational puzzles, pogo sticks, electric pianos, giant pandas, personal radios and television sets with which parents of even moderate means now smother infants. And this in spite of the fact that any experienced mother knows babies are democratic about toys. Hand them an empty oatmeal box and a spoon and they will contentedly beat time on that improvised drum. Give them pie plates to pound, a chain of buttons to finger, a barricade of kitchen chairs to make their way around, and no jungle gym amuses them more validly. But there is status involved. What the little Joneses have, all must have. A bicycle used to be an approximation, for a boy, of the exurbanite's Jaguar—a glittering dream acquired only after months of coaxing, saving up, delivering papers on a local route, or dropping hints to generous grandparents. When it arrived at last, some delirious Christmas or glorious birthday morning, the child marched like a monarch into his kingdom. Now bicycles come in so many sizes, appear so early on the juvenile scene, that a jaded owner has often possessed (or wrecked or lost) several by the time he learns long division. For him it has never been an achievement, merely an expected convenience, like his book bag or his winter snowsuit.

By the same token he has probably found his interest waning early in the complicated system of electric railroads his father bought him before he was old enough to know a culvert from a coupling. Familiarity breeds not only contempt but ennui.

The other day I saw three little boys ambling down a rural road. Young as they were, they knew the gambit of the thumb, and I obligingly stopped the car to pick them up. As they shambled into the back seat, each of them flicked off the transistor radio he had been carrying along on his nature walk. I was less amused than horrified. What was the excitement of exploring woods and rocks to these world-weary young Croesuses whose imaginative resources had grown so limited by riches that only an adult gadget could entertain them? It is little wonder that by adolescence such possession-drowned children have no dreams left to wait for and take to crashing parties or doing a bit of shoplifting in supermarkets by way of diversion.

When I think of riches I am reminded of dollhouses. Of all symbols of childhood (at least to me, who have only daughters) the dollhouse seems the most enduring. The little girl lucky enough to be given one used to be empress of her coterie. And eight years old used to be judged the proper age to become a chatelaine, as, indeed, it still is. Eight is house-proud. Eight arranges furniture, dusts the living room, sets Lilliputian tables, is as careful with her things as a Dutch housewife. She is not a destroyer but a guardian of her hearth. Yet in half the nurseries I enter nowadays, babies of three and four are already tearing to pieces the little dwellings they cannot yet appreciate. What will they have left to yearn for?

Our younger daughter, patly on her eighth birthday, received a dollhouse. Her clever father had constructed it himself in our basement over five hardworking months.

We knew at the time that the project was partly for ourselves, a labor of personal gratification. And it turned out to be the most rewarding busywork we ever embarked on. We were architects, contractors, interior decorators. All the windows opened and closed. There was a real staircase with a newel-post, fireplaces, bookshelves, a bathroom with its own tiny scales and towels. Lights turned on in every room by individual switches made from radio appliances. Everything was built to scale. The walls we papered with material designed for bookbinders, since ordinary wallpaper of even the smallest pattern loomed immoderately large. We covered the floors with upholstery fabrics, stretched and tacked by hand. There was a telephone. There was a grandfather clock. The doll's refrigerator bulged with food. I, who do not willingly sew on a button or put up a hem, spent weeks stitching tiny tablecloths and curtains. And of course the secret (for we managed somehow to keep it secret) was the greatest imaginable success. The birthday child eclipsed the grandest of the Joneses. She began to be courted even by little boys, who would not admit to being interested in anything concerning dolls but who professed, nevertheless, to admire the ingenious way you could press a button at the front door and hear a bell ring in that splendid house.

She loved it, naturally. She loves it still, and we store it now in the attic against the day her own daughter turns eight. Yet I think we gave her, again, too much too early. If we had let her paint her own walls, invent her own furniture, design her own curtains, however ill-made, the gift might have held a greater magic. Wealth can be stifling. The houses I made out of shoe boxes when *I* was eight, with their cardboard beds and pasted-up draperies and chairs concocted from acorn caps, afforded me more actual pleasure, I believe, than any child gets now from a prefabricated mansion. They made me a creator.

It is the fun of creation which today's overindulged children are in danger of missing.

I would tell all these things to novice parents if they would listen. I would beg them to hold off their well-meant efforts to provide the young with all joys and all accomplishments before their hands (or their hearts) were large enough to hold them. I would remind them that the copybook maxim still holds: Happiness is not manufactured from goods but from good. At the same time I would ask tolerance from them; tolerance of mediocrity, casual acceptance of their children's limitations as of their talents.

"Let them walk forward at their own speed," I would say. "Give love rather than possessions, moral standards rather than a sense of competition, an education fitted not to any arbitrary test or the ambitions of the Joneses, but to their individual and fledgling minds. Then, when success or failure comes, they will be better able to cope with it."

Surely on a planet increasingly chilly to the touch, uncomplicated childhood ought to remain the last warm and lighted house in which the human animal can shelter for a time while he grows strong enough to face the gathering winds of the world.

21 The Casual Touch

Somewhat to my astonishment a few weeks ago, I found myself lunching at one of those celebrity-haunted restaurants where one goes to stare rather than to dine. It was not my choice (I'm the Schrafft's chopped-chicken-on-nut-bread-and-fruit-salad type by habit) but an out-of-town friend had persuaded me to join her for veal scallopini —at a king's ransom—and a good look around. She hoped, I suppose, to carry back to Denver with her the enviable news that she had seen Walter Slezak waving to Jean Kerr at an adjoining table or Richard Burton discussing his next film. We encountered no recognizable lions, but I did see an appealing thing.

In a nearby booth an attractive blond young woman with the pad and pencil of a reporter was interviewing one of the *un*recognizable notables. She was animated, evidently experienced, and she was accompanied by a friend. The friend was a baby, surely not more than three or four months old, gurgling in a basket on the seat beside her. Every now and then she would lean over to pat him almost without thinking about it, and then go on with her conversation.

I was unable to overhear her explanation of why she had fetched him along, but I imagine it went something like this: "The maid couldn't come. We had this appointment. What could I do but bring the lad?"

"Pretty casual," murmured my luncheon companion.

"Pretty *and* casual," I corrected her, since no one in the restaurant seemed perturbed, least of all the baby. And I watched with admiration the little family's departure when the interview was over. The baby began to stir, no doubt agitated by memories of milk and pablum. He was promptly swung out of his basket and up to his mother's shoulder, bright head and fuzzy one bobbling together in tolerant communication. She said her good-byes to the Personage (to us nameless) and marched out as easily as if she had been carrying a bouquet, nodding to the headwaiter, smiling at friends, hailing a taxi at the door.

Wonderful, I thought to myself, choosing a Napoleon from the dessert cart. That's one young fellow who ought to grow up confident as Peter Pan. And there's a parent who's going to enjoy her children.

I suggested as much to my friend, who answered me a bit crossly. (After all, I had disappointed her. I hadn't produced so much as a platinum starlet making eyes at her agent.) She wanted to know what was so wonderful about carrying an infant around to cafés, when he'd have been better off in his own crib.

"It's not what she did," I tried to explain. "It's the casual way she did it. No apologies. No fuss. Remember what a production we used to make over sheltering our young ones? Well, I envy motherhood which can take itself lightly."

I felt myself working up to real eloquence. "Nothing better could happen to a child than to be treated offhandedly," I pontificated. "To be possessed without possessiveness—to be loved without hysterics . . ."

My friend cut off my philosophizing, for she had shopping on her agenda, and bore me off with her to find a New York Hat. We pursued the subject no further; but it had made an impression on my easily impressed mind. Sorting out my thoughts on the way to the station that evening, I came to a biased conclusion. There are, in the maternal catalog, dozens of dazzling virtues. But if I had to choose my favorite from the list—that long list which includes such high and heroic qualities as fortitude, patience, compassion, and self-sacrifice—I would single out a smaller one. I would choose casualness. It is the nicest, the healthiest of the lot. It is also the most rare.

There are a number of reasons for its rarity. Lightheartedness and strength of character are never common, and the casual touch demands both. It also requires self-confidence. But parents in this generation have had their confidence undermined by too many changes of doctrine, too much advice from contradictory sources. Mothers in other eras may have owned anxieties, but they were upheld by a simple creed. They felt that the mere fact of maternity bestowed on them a kind of infallibility. Mother, they were certain, knew best. They might consult the family physician about whooping cough or skin rashes. They might ask counsel from *their* mothers about making formulas or baby clothes. But when it came to matters of conduct, they consulted only their own hearts and inclinations. They had never heard of traumas or behavior patterns or listened to thunder from the mounts of psychiatry.

We in our time have listened to them all and been confused by them. In a little more than two decades I have seen the pediatric gospel alter several times. When my children were babies we were taught to live by schedule as commuters live by railroad timetables. Feeding-on-demand, for instance, was considered a scandal. We were sternly instructed that crying was good for babies' lungs and that we must not pick up hungry or wailing young just because they *were* wailing. Mothers being mortal, we habitually, of course, used to break the law. Few of us could bear to let lungs expand more than fifteen minutes at a time. But when we cosseted the weeper or fed him a half-hour early, we felt guilty as criminals. Toilet training began practically at birth, and we all kept charts and took temperatures and wrung our hands if Baby was recalcitrant about the potty or left even a quarter-ounce of milk unfinished in his bottle. It was nearly impossible to be casual with such a regime.

That pattern changed to demand-feeding and to diapers worn until the child himself rebelled. But anxieties went on because Authority kept insisting that parents were totally responsible for their progeny's every deviation from an imaginary norm. Children must not only be healthy. They must also be happy, popular, and well-adjusted. If they weren't, mothers had somehow failed. Heredity was dismissed as incidental. Nobody gave excuse to human accident. Authority was our conscience, and it made cowards of us all.

What we were not told—and what parents to this day are insufficiently warned—is that all rules are meant to be broken now and then, that children are not statistics, and that the important thing for a mother to cultivate is a forgiving nature. Over and over she must learn to forgive herself.

Casualness does exactly that.

"There's one thing Fred and I have decided," said a sensible acquaintance of mine recently, the mother of six delightful children whom she treats firmly but with insouciance. "We realize we have a duty to our bunch. It's up to us to get them educated and fed and clothed and taught morals. It's not our duty, though, to make them be happy. That's *their* job."

All parents on the planet might sleep better at night if they agreed with her. Their offspring, too, might breathe more freely. That rugged sextet reared on love, orders, and an occasional spanking have an excellent chance of growing up in tune with a personal universe, liberated as they are by her watchful but lenient regard from the obligation of being "successes."

For let me make it plain that when I speak of casualness, I do not mean carelessness. (The little interviewer with her portable baby was not being careless—quite the contrary. She might have called in a strange sitter for the sake of convenience and of leaving her son in his accustomed bed. Instead, she gave him the security of herself, a far more reliable rampart than his nursery walls.) Actually, I have known few careless mothers. I have met their young, roaming at large in our village, wandering into our kitchen at mealtimes, straggling home after dark down suburban streets. I have now and then fished them out of deep water at the beach. But in the circles I inhabit, we are not given to neglect. We are apt to be permissive instead, which is also a different thing from being casual.

I remember still the patient, the wistful voice of a woman sitting next to me in the park not so long ago.

"Mother wishes you wouldn't," she was repeating monotonously to her frail four-year-old. "Mother doesn't *like* to be hit in the head with a dump truck."

The casual mother would have seen the dump truck coming and calmly confiscated it. Even I, in my benighted day, owned one abiding faith—that I was brighter and a good deal stronger than any four-year-old. If anybody got bruises from lethal toys around our house, it wasn't going to be me. Nor did I make the mistake of consulting underaged opinion on vital matters, as did a friend of mine. Every Christmas she used to ask her small (and only) son if he would like to have a tree. Since "no" is easier to say than "yes," he inevitably used the negative, so angels and tinsel were banished from their holidays.

"I do wish Lionel would change his mind," she told me plaintively once when she found me laying out strings of lights. "I'd love just one Christmas to trim an evergreen." And it was not until Lionel was grown up that she discovered he had resented all through his childhood the fact they did not celebrate like other people. He simply had not wanted to shoulder repsonsibility himself.

The casual mother takes it for granted that normal children will enjoy normal treats. She gives them Christmas trees as she gives them bananas and coloring books and vitamins, each in what seems to her the proper season. On the other hand, she is not put off if they spurn the fruit or forget an occasional pill or refuse to share her delight in carol singing. She has either learned or knows in her bones that every creature in the world is a singular individual with individual preferences. Her children are not herself. She has borne them, endowed them with chromosomes and genes, shaped them by example. They are still unique and different from her, with varying talents, aspirations, quirks, and dispositions. So she does not mound them into following her particular bent. The dreamer is permitted his dreams, the extrovert his sports and gregarious comrades. There is no set goal, except good behavior, which every member of the family must attain—or be aware he has disappointed her.

She does not nag, and she argues very little. She does not have to be told, as I was by an eight-year-old daughter, that argument defeats itself at times. "Oh, Mommie," she burst out once when I was reasoning with her over some childish lapse, "why don't you just tell me not to, and stop *explaining* at me?" Casualness prefers, to argument, its own brand of discipline.

It is a light and comfortable discipline, invented not for the pleasure of passing laws but for the comfort of the household. Rules are simple, few, and easy to put on as bedroom slippers. Nothing is asked beyond the child's abilities, the family needs, and the demands of good taste. (Sloth is discouraged like self-pity, bad posture like bubble gum—and for the same good reason, that they are vulgar.) He may be expected to pick himself up without tears at three, and at five, still stoic, to pick up his toys. He takes himself punctually back and forth to school, perhaps, at seven; stables his bicycle at nine; feeds his own pets and helps with the gardening or the garbage or the younger children at ten; and at fourteen (or at twenty) lives within his allowance. Whatever tasks he is asked to perform are useful ones, not busywork. He is neither oppressed nor overindulged, merely treated like one reliable member of an organized group, each with his own portion to deliver of labor and responsibility.

Whoever wears such a discipline feels at once free and protected. To him it is not a thong but a garment. Sometimes he even forgets he has it on.

I saw an amusing example of that forgetfulness when I dined out (at another restaurant and an even more impressive one) last year with the nonchalant parents of three strapping young men. They all live in the country, where domestic help is hard to come by, so the boys have learned to lend a hand at the dinner table.

"All right, men, clear away," says the lady of the house at the end of the meal, and all three young males ungrudgingly carry out the plates and bring in the coffee.

This night they were relaxing in the unaccustomed splendor of being served by ambidextrous waiters and of ordering glorious dishes with French names. We were planning to get to the theater after dinner, so we hurried them a little, suggesting that *crêpes Suzette* might take too much time and couldn't they settle for a pastry, instead? At eight-twenty, we decided there really was an emergency if we were to make the curtain, so we called for the bill.

"All right, men," ordered the mother briskly, meaning only, "Let's get this show on the road."

But at the familiar signal, each of the three boys, to the diversion of every diner in the room, automatically picked up his dishes and started marching with them toward the kitchen.

In a less-emancipated family (one where rules were not allowed to explode in one's face), someone might have wilted with embarrassment. Instead we all left in such an atmosphere of laughter and good humor that what turned out to be a mediocre musical entertained as well as if it had been *My Fair Lady*. The boys were mocked, but with fondness.

For casual mothers are quite as fond as tense ones. Calmness is not ice. Actually, the mothers I praise give their love more generously than the rest of us, since it is a free gift without strings attached.

One of the human difficulties is to keep our noblest of emotions within bounds. Love can be a sustaining fountain or it can drown like a torrent. I have seen children struggling like flood victims in their parents' smothering affections. Casualness disciplines its love as it disciplines its home. Love with a casual touch never says, "My children are my life." That mother makes a life of her own which is full enough and rewarding enough to sustain her. And she permits her young to let *their* lives be individual accomplishments.

What she chiefly does is respect her offspring. She does not snoop and she forbears to pry. She can keep a child's secret even from herself, and she would no more open his mail or read his diary than she would steal from his piggy bank. Because her family trusts her, she is more apt to receive confidences than are lesser women. But unreceived ones she can also handle. She just says, "Oh, that John is a clam!" and goes on letting him be as clamlike as is necessary to his ego. Her fondness is full of charity and covers a multitude of deficiencies.

It does not, however, make her into a victim. She is capable of self-sacrifice, but to it she prefers self-fulfillment, which is safer for everybody concerned. There is an old folktale which she would despise if she ever heard it, although it has been told and retold by sentimentalists as an example of true motherhood.

There was once a widow with an only son. He was a handsome and promising boy for whom she delighted to expend herself. His happiness was her sole ambition, and she did indeed keep him comfortable and happy until he grew up into a beautiful young man. Then, as beautiful young men are inclined to do, he fell in love. But the girl of his choice hated the mother because her shadow fell between them. So she said to the youth, "If you really love me, you will give me everything. Bring me your mother's jewels."

"My beloved must have your jewels," he said to his mother. And since her only object was to make him happy, she brought out her few brooches and cameos, and he took them to the girl.

Still the wicked young woman was not satisfied. She said to him, "If you really love me, you will give me everything. Let me live in your mother's house."

So the boy turned his mother out of her house. And because her only object was to make him happy, she went willingly to live in a hut in the forest.

Still the enchantress was not satisfied. "If you really love me, you will give me everything," she said at last. "Bring me your mother's heart."

And the boy went to his mother, who, because to see him happy was her only object, gave him her heart.

As he was running to the girl, with the heart still warm and palpitating in his hands, he stumbled on a stone and fell. Then the heart, which all this time had kept silent over its own sufferings, cried out piteously, "Have you hurt yourself, my son?"

Now that's quite a touching story, and if you tell it with the right inflection it doesn't leave a dry eye in the audience. It has a moral, too, but I don't believe it's the one the inventor of the tale intended. All it proves to me is the stupidity of doting mothers.

The casual type would have laughed the boy off her premises if he had come to her with such ridiculous demands.

"You want to give her a ring? You need an apartment? Get a job, young man. As for my heart, I expect to need it myself for some time to come."

And she would have put a stop to that dandy little misalliance in an afternoon. In fact, since he was his mother's son, I don't think it would have happened in the first place.

22 ❧ *The Last Word*

Good things incline to come in threes. It is the most familiar and benign of trios which I have discussed, however lightly, in this book. Wifehood, the house, a family; they are woman's traditional concern and each in its way represents one of the other great three—faith, hope, charity—which St. Paul sets down as the virtues of earth. (For how can one rear a family without faith? Or build a roof without hope? Or remain a proper wife without charity?) They are life's vital elements and no ordered world can endure without them.

Is it not astonishing, then, how little they are taken into account when sociologists foregather?

The experts speak about everything else concerning the feminine race except the reason we exist. They argue our wrongs but forget our ancient rights. They debate our stature as voters, job-holders, wage-earners, citizens of the state. As mothers and wives, we are given scarcely the dignity of a paragraph. They are concerned (quite rightly) with our working conditions in factories. As workers in the home we are issued few bulletins. They plan the correct size of our families while omitting any reference to the morality and happiness of families already in our care.

In such a context, we become less than women, creatures no different from men except for our civic disabilities.

Yet women, no matter how emancipated, are *not* men. We belong to separate nations. Our pulses beat to a different rhythm, our aspirations and rewards are dissimilar. We do not feel like men or think like men or, except under special circumstances, act like our opposite numbers. One in every three American workers may be female; and, quite rightly, the welfare of those workers ought to be guarded. Equal pay for equal services is an important and urgent bit of legislation. But it is not only as salaried employees or hired hands that women function most often or most profitably. Talk as the pundits will about our contribution to industry or the sciences or the arts (and the air is noisy with their talk), it is as mothers and wives and householders that we make our unique contribution to humanity.

A reactionary attitude? Not at all. Merely realistic. Far more realistic, I maintain, than that popular one struck recently by the new feminists among us. They would have us believe that all the ills of society and most of our own spring from our craven running back to the safety of the hearth. Women have a chance at last, they declare, to become men—without the "woe," as it were—and we are flinging it away. All professional roads are open to us. But we insist willfully on returning to the ancient, well-trodden trail which leads merely to the domestic door. We have too many babies. We take too much pride in being good cooks, in keeping immaculate houses. So we are turning into neurotics and weeping into our bread as we bake it.

Well, it may be there are neurotics among us, and we certainly weep now and then, as women always have, over griefs and disappointments. What the authors of these screeds do not take into account is that full-time housewives are no more apt to turn hysterical than is the unhappy secretary to a corporation head, and are even less likely to become alcoholics or to indulge in depressions than is the hard-driven lady copywriter for an advertising agency. Besides, this age breeds neuroses as other eras ran to plagues and fires. We live on a threatened planet. Since we are the thinking reeds of the universe, we cannot help contemplating the world; so that, to misquote Housman, we

> . . . think by fits and starts.
> And if we think, we fasten
> Our hands upon our hearts.

Desperation is the human condition. But it is no more the condition of the housewife than of women in general —and of men also, which is another thing the writers of those feminists books forget. Not all hardworking husbands are happy in their professions, not all male jobholders are successful or delighted with their lots. The hypochondriacs, the takers of sleeping pills or Benzedrine tablets, the drinkers, the despairers—according to statistics, they are even more apt to be male than female. And it is this truth, that the public role is not an all-satisfying one, which many sensible women are discovering. Their commercial skills and talents will not of necessity make them any more delighted with life when exercised in the marketplace than when placed casually on a kitchen counter. If they can combine the two sorts of work, well and good. If not, they feel they are opting for the more exciting part when they polish the hearth. That, and not a death wish or or a strange urge toward self-immolation, has persuaded them back to their antique occupation.

They know (either by instinct or by observation) that the home is the world's end and its beginning—and that only women can properly create it. A perceptive writer who has not always praised the modern women is the anthropologist Margaret Mead. Yet she, in a recent article discussing the results of the President's Commission on the Status of Women, has this to say concerning the home-centered career:

"Through the ages, human beings have remained human because there were women whose duty it was to provide continuity in their lives—to be there when they went to sleep and when they woke up, to ease pain, to sympathize with failure and rejoice at success, to listen to tales of broken hearts, to soothe and support and sustain and stimulate husbands and sons as they faced the vicissitudes of a hard outside world. . . . The young, the sick, the old, the unhappy and the triumphantly victorious have needed special individuals to share with them and care for them."

It is her conclusion that not too many but too few women keep their status as full-time housewives. Whether full-time or in part, however, the keeper of the home is the most important woman in the world. That willingness to "support and sustain and stimulate," to make an atmosphere in which the larger, if not the more vital, affairs of earth can get accomplished is singular to our sex. We should feel honored to have this dispensation in our hands. For both those who give it and those who take it, it is the soul's chief nourishment.

I have sung, then, and continue to sing the worth of a

domestic career in an age where it is terribly needed. We crave light and warmth in this century. Only the mother, the wife, can supply it for the home. To be a housewife is not easy. Ours is a difficult, a wrenching, sometimes an ungrateful job if it is looked on only as a job. Regarded as a profession, it is the noblest as it is the most ancient of the catalog. Let none persuade us differently or the world is lost indeed.

A WREATH OF RECIPES

Let's get this straight at the beginning. I talk a very good meal.

That is, while I do cook, and cook well enough to please my family, regale my friends, and raise my self-esteem, I am not a professional chef. My repertoire is neither enormous nor particularly original, and I am capable of making mistakes like everybody else. There are kitchen secrets I have not yet discovered, accomplishments beyond my skill.

But I am a willing, a constant learner. I pore over cookbooks. I study techniques, coax recipes from my cronies, and accept advice from acquaintances on improving our family table. And over the years, I have built up an accumulation of recipes which have been repeatedly and successfully tested on the household. It is these which I pass along now to such readers as may be interested.

But I pass them on for a reason more important than the urge of one cook to chat with another. I feel I might be cheating if I do not list them.

For there are certain nettling books which irritate me beyond mortal measure. Perhaps you too have been maddened by them. There you are, gliding raptly through a novel or an autobiography or a collection of essays, only to be brought up short by the author's unfairness. He describes with gusto some celestial-sounding food for which he gives no recipe. Your salivary juices are aroused, your curiosity stimulated. But you have no notion at all how you might go down to your stove and set about preparing that dish.

When, therefore, I looked over this manuscript, I decided to play more fairly with readers than do the writers I fulminate against. I append here a collection of sixteen recipes for food which I have either recommended or described in foregoing chapters. (If I were to give the directions for every one I have spoken of merely in passing, this book would turn out fatter than the Manhattan telephone directory.)

None of them is difficult. I commend them all. And I trust that if you try them, you will eat the results with a good appetite and in a cheerful spirit.

Beef and Vegetable One-dish Soup

This is one of the most delicious single-dish meals in the world, and it is something you could serve your most sophisticated guests with pride. It sounds complicated and as if it were a great deal of work, but really it is not. What it does demand is time. You must plan to spend two days on its making. You must also be on good terms with your butcher so he will supply you with the right meats and bones. And you need a very large soup kettle.

1 shank of beef with meat still on bone
1 veal knuckle
Several chicken feet, or if those are not obtainable,
several chicken necks
3 or 4 pounds of beef rump in a chunk

All the beef bones your butcher can spare you—pounds and pounds of them. (It is the bones which give the soup its rich consistency. Make sure there are marrow-bones among them.)
1 large white turnip, cut up, or 3 small ones
1 parsnip
Several leeks
1 good-sized onion, cut up
2 cloves of garlic, diced or passed through a garlic press
3 or 4 whole cloves
2 tomatoes, unpeeled
2 or 3 tablespoons tomato catsup
Dash lemon juice
6 stalks of celery, leaves and all, diced
Handful of parsley
4 cans beef consommé
1 teaspoon dried rosemary
½ small green cabbage
Potatoes
Carrots
Handful of green beans and shelled peas
Enough water to cover all

Wash bones and place them at bottom of kettle. Add chicken feet or necks, turnip, parsnip, leeks, onion, catsup, tomato, lemon juice, parsley, half the celery, and the rosemary. Add the beef rump. Put in the beef consommé. Fill the kettle with water enough to cover ingredients. Place lid on kettle and bring to boil, skimming off scum as it appears. When all is boiling merrily, turn heat to simmer and cook for four to five hours. At end of that time, remove the meat and put it aside for the next day. Continue cooking bones and vegetables for the rest of the day—I like to give it at least eight hours.

Remove from stove, cool until it is possible to handle the kettle without danger of scalding yourself, strain through colander into another kettle. Then do an extravagant thing. Throw away all the cooked-out vegetables and flavoring. The bones you can give to your dog or use for compost in your garden.

The next day, two or three hours before you wish to serve the soup, take the broth out of the refrigerator. It ought, if you have cooked it long enough, to be congealed to the consistency of a very firm jelly. Now skim off *all* the fat. Place kettle of greaseless soup on stove and add to it the carrots, the beans, the rest of the celery, and the potatoes which you will eat that night. After half an hour of simmering, add cabbage and peas. Add the beef just long enough to heat it through. When it *is* heated, remove it to a warm platter and slice as you would a pot roast. Then pour the soup itself, along with its gleaming vegetables, into a tureen. Bring to the table and ladle into large soup plates. Pass the sliced beef. With this shining dark-brown garden-scented treat, serve hot, crisp French bread and, if you like, a green salad. Nothing else. It is a feast for peasant or for king.

Dried Beef and Mushrooms

½ pound dried beef bought in bulk, not in a glass jar
½ pound fresh mushrooms or 1 can sliced cooked mushrooms

3 tablespoons flour
3 tablespoons butter
2 ½ cups milk
Good strong dash ground black pepper
1 tablespoon onion juice

Make a cream sauce from flour and butter, first browning the butter so it will not be pallid. If mushrooms are fresh, sauté them lightly and add to cream sauce along with onion juice. If they are canned, simply put them into sauce. I sometimes add the juice in which they come to the cream sauce for extra flavor.

Now pour over the beef enough boiling water just to cover it. Pour off immediately. This takes away enough of the salt from the cured beef so that it is tangy but appetizing. When you have drained it, pull the meat apart with your fingers, shredding it into fairly fine wisps. There is nothing less appealing than hunks of it stirred into the sauce.

Add desalted beef to sauce, bring all to a boil, and let simmer just a few minutes. Season with ground black pepper. If you have taken *too* much salt away, by letting the beef soak too long, you might try adding not salt but a bit of beef extract. It makes a heartier dish and adds color to it. Serve on toast from which crusts have been cut.

You can vary this recipe by adding other ingredients to the sauce, such as green pepper, celery (diced), water chestnuts, or hard-boiled egg.

Savory Cabbage

1 head young green cabbage
2 tablespoons butter
¼ sweet apple, sliced
1 teaspoon caraway seeds
1 tablespoon boiling water
Salt and pepper to taste

Cut cabbage into quarters. Carve out hard core and discard. Place quarters of cabbage, cut side down, on chopping board and slice as thin as your nice sharp knife can manage.

Melt butter in saucepan until it is hot but not brown, add boiling water, cabbage, and apple. Season with salt and pepper. Fix lid on pan as tightly as possible and simmer or steam for fifteen or twenty minutes or until just tender. Add caraway seeds and serve at once.

Braised Chicken Hearts

Hearts of chickens are delicious and cheap. When I cook them, I usually add a few chicken livers, but it is important to make sure the livers cook less long than the tougher hearts.

Melt two to three tablespoons of butter in a heavy frying pan. Add a pound or so of hearts, salted and peppered and dusted with flour. Add half a medium onion, diced fine. Cover and cook slowly until hearts are tender.

These can be served exactly like this. Or, if you prefer, you can make a sauce for them. Add to the pan in which they cook one tablespoon flour and one cup chicken broth. Add two tablespoons of sour cream. Bring to a boil and serve immediately with toast or simply as an unadorned entrée.

Boiled Custard

A soft boiled custard is not just a dish in itself; it is the basis for dozens of delightful desserts, such as floating island, pôt de crème, trifle, and so on. The secret in making it smooth, perfect, and uncurdled lies in never letting the water boil in the bottom of the double boiler and in using a candy thermometer.

Yolks of six eggs, beaten yellow but not dry
¼ cup white or brown sugar
⅛ teaspoon salt
2 cups scalded milk
Vanilla or sherry to taste

To the beaten egg yolks, add sugar, salt, and milk. Cook and stir over low heat in a double boiler. The water must never bubble into a boil. When the custard is cooked to 175 degrees by the thermometer, it is done and must be taken off the stove, flavored, and put aside to use.

If you do not own a candy thermometer, watch the stirring spoon. When it coats all over with the egg mixture and nothing drips from it, the 175 degrees has been reached.

Baking-powder Dumplings for Stew

1 cup flour
2 teaspoons baking powder

½ teaspoon sugar
½ teaspoon salt
¼ to ½ cup milk
2 tablespoons butter or other shortening
1 well-beaten egg
1 tablespoon chopped parsley
Pinch nutmeg

Sift together flour, baking powder, sugar, and salt. Dot mixture with butter and cut together with two knives or pastry cutter. In other words, treat the batter as you would biscuits or pie dough. Add beaten egg, parsley, and nutmeg. Then, making a hole at the bottom of the mixture, slowly add milk until batter holds together but is stiff and not damp.

If you have a steamer, drop the mixture by rounded spoonfuls onto its slightly buttered surface. If you don't have a steamer, use the stew itself as a surface, but make sure no liquid touches the dumplings. The meat and potatoes must sit above the gravy and form a protection for the pastry, and the water or broth must be boiling when your delicacies are dropped from the spoon.

Arrange fairly close together, put lid on pot, and cook for twenty minutes without removing the cover. Serve around the stew. If correctly steamed, your dumplings should emerge light as a ballet dancer's leap, a feast not even the dieter can resist.

Potato Dumplings

2 pounds potatoes
½ cup flour
1 egg
Salt, pepper, and nutmeg to taste
Deep pan full of boiling salted water or broth
Bread croutons

Boil the potatoes in their jackets. Peel and mash, using no liquid. Add flour and beaten egg. Flavor with salt, pepper, nutmeg. Chill for one hour.

When mixture is cold, take from refrigerator and form into balls, each around a large crouton of bread. Dust with flour. Drop into boiling liquid, lower heat, and cook, uncovered, about five or six minutes. Remove with slotted spoon and serve on separate plate with *Sauerbraten.*

Note of Warning: These are tricky to cook, since potato balls sometimes disintegrate in water. Try one to begin with. If it does not cook whole, add more flour to other balls. And if you simply cannot get them to cook correctly, throw out your hot water and sauté the dumplings in brown butter. They will turn out to be croquettes, a pleasant accompaniment to a roast, if not quite the traditional dish.

Hazelnut Roll

6 eggs
¾ cup sugar

1½ cups chopped hazelnuts (done in blendor if you have one); hazelnuts are the best for this dessert, but walnuts or chopped pecans will do
1 teaspoon baking powder
Few grains salt
1½ cups heavy Cream
Rum or vanilla to taste

Separate eggs and beat whites until they stand in soft peaks. Beat half a cup of sugar into mixture and set aside. Without washing beater, beat yolks until thick and lemon-colored. Beat into them the remaining sugar.
Mix chopped nuts, baking powder, salt. Stir into egg-yolk mixture. Fold in the beaten whites. Spread batter evenly into a jelly-roll pan about 10 x 14 inches which has been buttered, lined with waxed paper, and rebuttered over the paper. Place in center of preheated oven set at 350 degrees. Bake twenty minutes. Take out of oven and cover with damp towel. Chill.
When you wish to add cream, take cake out of refrigerator, peel off the waxed paper and cut off crisp ends. Spread whipped cream (to which sugar and rum have been added) evenly over cake. Roll like a jelly roll. Wrap firmly in waxed paper and rechill. This can oven be put into the freezer and used later. Cut in slices or bring to table on long platter. I have now and then tried frosting the whole roll with whipped cream but it is really too rich that way. A little powdered sugar is all that is necessary by way of garnish.

Molded Peach Pudding

1 package orange gelatin
1 cup hot peach juice
1 cup canned peaches
½ cup port wine, Marsala, or peach liqueur
½ cup whipping cream
Several fresh peaches, sliced, or 1 package frozen peaches

Dissolve gelatin in hot liquid from canned peaches. Cool to lukewarm. Place canned peaches, well drained, gelatin mixture, and wine in electric blendor. Cover container and beat, first at low speed, then at high, until all is thoroughly mixed and smooth. Add cream and whip for a few seconds only. Pour into mold and chill until firm.
When you wish to serve this pretty and tasty dessert, carefully unmold and garnish with fresh or frozen peaches.

Frozen Peas, French Style

I am one of those people who do not subscribe to the popular belief that frozen vegetables taste just as good as fresh ones. On the contrary, I think most of them taste like nothing at all except the cardboard container. But now and then I use commercially iced products and by dint of seasoning them strongly and coaxing them along with cream and butter make an adequate dish for gracing a winter table. One of them is this chic casserole.

1 package frozen peas
1 head Boston lettuce

1 clove garlic, passed through garlic press
Several small onions or 1 medium-sized one, sliced thin
2 tablespoons butter
1 tablespoon hot water
Pinch flour
1 teaspoon rosemary
2 or 3 sprigs parsley
1 teaspoon sugar
Salt and pepper to taste

In a heavy, lidded skillet, place half the lettuce, arranging the leaves like a nest. Add rest of ingredients except peas. Put on heavy lid. Bring to a boil, turn down heat, and simmer very slowly for half an hour. Add peas. Add rest of lettuce, making a green tent over the vegetable. Bring once more to a boil, reduce to simmer, and cook slowly for half an hour longer, always covered.

If you do not like the looks of the cooked lettuce, be finicky. Fish it laboriously out of the pan. Personally, I like the taste of the lettuce itself and serve it, bedraggled as it is apt to appear. There should be very little liquid left in the pan, and that ought to be fairly thick. If you like, you can add more butter or a little heavy cream. Serve mixture in a warmed dish.

A Foolproof Recipe for Piecrust

3 cups of plain all-purpose flour
1 heaping cup of shortening, chilled
1 teaspoon salt

1 teaspoon sugar
1 pinch of double-action baking powder (if you do not know how to measure a "pinch," try using half of a quarter teaspoon)
6 scanty tablespoons of very cold water
Large mixing bowl
Two table knives
One ordinary table fork
A pastry cutter
A pastry cloth
Rolling pin and knitted sleeve
A 9- or 10-inch pie plate
A pair of sharp scissors
Waxed paper

Sift into a bowl, once and all together, the flour, salt, sugar, and baking powder. Add the shortening in lumps. With two knives (one in each hand, held at right angles to each other), cut through the flour and shortening until it is partly mixed together. Then continue cutting it with the pastry cutter until the mixture resembles coarse oatmeal.

At this stage, add the cold water, one spoonful at a time. Sprinkle over the dough and stir gently with the fork, bringing the fork up from the bottom of the bowl. If the day is moist or rainy, add less water, but never add more. It is too much water which toughens the crust.

After the mixture becomes coherent, dump the whole thing out onto a large piece of waxed paper and fold the paper over it. You will think to yourself, "This stuff does not hold together. It will never roll." But you are wrong. After you have delicately patted the dough underneath the waxed paper, it will cling together very nicely.

Then unfold the paper and let the pastry slide onto a floured pastry cloth. Stretch the sleeve over the rolling pin and flour *that.* Begin to roll away from the center of the dough, in long, gentle motions, to the rim of the pastry. Press lightly on the rolling pin, for piecrust is not an enemy to be attacked but a friend to be treated with consideration.

When you have rolled it as thin as you like, hold a pie pan over the dough and cut out a circle of pastry large enough to fit the pan with about an inch of overlap around the edges. Scissors are useful for trimming, since they cut better than a knife. An easy way to transfer the pastry to the pan is to roll it around the rolling pin like a coiling serpent, then carefully unroll it again onto the receptacle. Otherwise it may break and you will have to piece the dough—a trying job.

Fill the shell you have made with whatever filling you plan to use, and again repeat the process of rolling, cutting, and coiling for the top crust. Then press the edges of the two crusts together with your fingers and tweak the overlapping crust into a fluting around the rim of the pan. The amount of fluting is left to your artistic devices. One thing you *must* do, however, is to prick the surface of the top crust well into the pastry with a fork, so that the steam can escape while the pie is cooking.

The oven should be set at 400 degrees (preheated for about ten minutes) and maintained at this temperature for the first fifteen or twenty minutes. Then, if the pie is browning too quickly, turn the heat down to a moderate 350. The average pie takes from fifty minutes to an hour to brown and bake.

The measurements I have given will make a piecrust and a half—that is, one shell and a fully covered pie. I write out the recipe in these dimensions because the quantity is so easy and accurate. The leftover pastry can be used in a number of delightful ways.

I often turn it into canapés. For example, buy a can or two of tiny skinless pork sausages and wrap each sausage in a little open-ended blanket of crust. When you want to serve them, fetch them out of the refrigerator or the freezer and bake them for from twenty minutes to half an hour in a moderate oven until they are delicately browned.

Or else roll the pastry out with grated cheese, slice it into thin strips, and bake those in a pie plate for ten or fifteen minutes. Both recipes are very good with cocktails.

Blendor Hollandaise Sauce

3 egg yolks
2½ tablespoons lemon juice
1 sprig parsley
Dash freshly ground black pepper
½ cup butter at room temperature
¼ cup boiling water

Place all ingredients except water in blendor. Cover and turn machine to medium speed. When ingredients are well mixed, remove top, and with the blendor running, gradually pour in boiling water. Run until contents are thoroughly blended, about one minute. Heat, stirring constantly, over hot (never boiling) water until the sauce is the consistency of custard.

This sauce will not only keep for the day in a double boiler but can be placed in the refrigerator and rewarmed later by leaving it at room temperature for a few hours. It is not quite so rich as regular hollandaise but it is foolproof, easy, and very good with almost any green vegetable.

Sauce Béarnaise

To already prepared hollandaise sauce, add a teaspoon finely chopped parsley and a teaspoon chopped fresh tarragon or a half tablespoon tarragon vinegar. Or make hollandaise with tarragon vinegar instead of lemon juice and add the fresh, chopped parsley.

Sauerbraten

This dish is truly German—echt Deutsch—and has the best German qualities. That is, it is robust, humorous, spicy, and slightly sentimental. I serve it not more than once a year, and then only in cold weather, and I plan for it several days ahead of time. I also make sure to have it for guests who are likely to consume it in one dining session. It is too singular in taste and too hearty to use as a leftover.

4-pound pot roast (eye of round or bottom round is the best cut)
Salt to taste
Several whole peppercorns
1 cup red wine or mild vinegar

1 large onion, thinly sliced
2 bay leaves
2 tablespoons sugar
Mixed spices, from 2 to 3 tablespoons (these can be nutmeg, cinnamon, mace, allspice, ginger, or anything your fancy turns to—perhaps you might settle for commercially mixed spices)
6 gingersnaps, crushed
½ cup sour cream
Enough boiling water mixed with beef consommé to cover roast

Place roast in deep bowl made of glass or pottery. Sprinkle around it rest of ingredients with the exception of water, gingersnaps, and sour cream. When it is nicely flavored, add mixed hot water and consommé, just enough to cover roast. Place lid on bowl and put into refrigerator for at least three days, preferably longer. Turn several times a day, using two wooden spoons or else your clean hands.

At end of marinating time, take meat out of bowl, brown well, and cook as you would cook any pot roast, using some of the strained liquid in which it has been soaking up its spicy goodness. Do not, however, drown it in liquid. A cup or two of the marinade is sufficient to begin with, and you can add more as the roast cooks if you require extra gravy.

When meat is tender but not dry, take it from container and skim broth of all grease. (You can do this by cooking the dish early in the day and chilling the broth, or you can dump a tray of ice cubes into the hot liquid to congeal the fat.) Put back on the stove and add to the liquid the crushed gingersnaps. Stir until smooth. Add, slowly, the sour cream.

Serve with potato dumplings, red cabbage and hot bread.

Sole, Shrimp, and Lobster Casserole

2 pounds sole or flounder filets
2 cans frozen shrimp soup, defrosted to room temperature
1 cup cooked lobster meat, fresh or frozen
2 tablespoons grated Parmesan cheese
1 tablespoon butter
1 tablespoon sherry, if desired, thickened with ½ tablespoon flour

Place filets of fish in shallow, buttered baking pan. Spread over them the defrosted soup, which ought to be smooth as custard. The bits of shrimp in it must be gently pressed underneath the fish and the soup; otherwise they will turn tough from heat. Add flour and sherry. Dust the Parmesan cheese over all. Dot with butter. Bake for twenty-five to thirty minutes in a preheated 375 degree oven.

Remove from oven and place pieces of lobster attractively around the edges of the baking pan, under the bubbling sauce. Return to oven and cook for five minutes longer. Or instead, if you like, you can put the casserole under a preheated broiler for five minutes. That broiling gives the cheese sauce a fine golden-brown touch.

The wine can be left out if you prefer and no flour added at all. Or in place of the extra lobster meat, you can add one cup cooked shrimp. As a matter of fact, this is a dish you can add to or subtract from as your fancy chooses. The only basic ingredients in it are the filets and the frozen soup.

Savory Sauce for Potatoes

⅛ pound butter
3 dessert spoons olive oil
Grated rind of 1 lemon
Juice of 1 lemon
Handful chopped fresh parsley
Chopped chives to taste
Dash nutmeg
Pinch flour
Salt and pepper to taste

Melt butter in a saucepan. *Do not brown.* Add olive oil and grated lemon rind. Add parsley, chives, nutmeg, flour, salt, and pepper—and be lavish with the pepper. Heat but do not bring to a boil. When ready to serve, add lemon juice and pour over potatoes.

This is an odd and delightful sauce for small new potatoes which have been cooked in their jackets and peeled while piping hot.

About the Author

Phyllis McGinley calls *Sixpence in Her Shoe* a "kind of autobiography . . . since the experiences I have drawn on are largely my own." And she remarks that the domestic profession is her "first vocation. But her second, that of writer, has produced nine volumes of verse, fifteen books for children, and a collection of essays. It has also won her such awards as the Pulitzer Prize for Poetry in 1960, the 1964 Laetare Medal given annually by the University of Notre Dame to a man or woman who has "enriched the heritage of humanity," and nearly a dozen honorary degrees—including one from that stronghold of strictly masculine pride, Dartmouth College.

Miss McGinley is married to Charles Hayden and has two daughters now grown up. The family, whom one meets at every charming turn in this book, lived for many years in a roomy Victorian house in Larchmont, New York, a village Miss McGinley has celebrated in both prose and verse. As a matter of fact, it is the setting for *Sixpence*.

Mr. and Mrs. Hayden have moved recently to a "new" two-hundred-and-twenty-year-old house in Weston, Connecticut.

發行人：周　政
住　址：台北市中山北路二段一八〇號
發行所：鍾　山　書　店
總經銷：中　山　書　店
地　址：台北市中山北路二段一八〇號
印刷所：華　南　印　製　廠
地　址：三重市正義北路二十八號
中華民國五十四年　月　日

登記證內版台業字第一〇三四號